Adoption Support Services for Families in Difficulty
A Literature Review and UK Survey

British Association for Adoption & Fostering
(BAAF)
Skyline House
200 Union Street
London SE1 0LX
www.baaf.org.uk

Charity registration 275689

British Library Cataloguing in Publication Data
A catalogue record for this book is available
from the British Library

ISBN 1 903699 15 0

Cover photographs by John Birdsall
Photography; posed by models
Designed by Andrew Haig & Associates
Typeset by Avon DataSet, Bidford on Avon
Printed by Russell Press Ltd (TU), Nottingham

BAAF Adoption & Fostering is the leading
UK-wide membership organisation for all those
concerned with adoption, fostering and child
care issues.

Adoption Support Services for Families in Difficulty
A Literature Review and UK Survey

Alan Rushton and Cherilyn Dance

Acknowledgements

We wish to thank the Nuffield Foundation for funding this research, and especially Sharon Witherspoon, the Deputy Director, who helped to initiate the project. We are also grateful to the key individuals who were so helpful to us in constructing the interview schedule. We also wish to express our appreciation to Claire Grace-Thorn, Debbie Alnock, Jane Harrison and Jessica Bjorklund for their help with interviewing respondents and searching for and collating references. Thanks are due to the agencies and key respondents who willingly gave their time to the study, and to our colleagues working in the adoption field who commented so constructively on the draft text.

Note about the authors

Alan Rushton, Senior Lecturer in Social Work, Institute of Psychiatry
Alan was for many years a mental health social worker with children and adults in the UK and in Canada, and currently directs the MSc programme in Mental Health Social Work. He has conducted research into a range of social work topics including adoption and fostering, child protection and post-qualifying training. He has authored several books and journal articles.

Cherilyn Dance, Freelance Researcher
Cherilyn has a background in child health and a degree in developmental psychology. For over ten years, she has been involved in research into adoption and fostering and was part of the Maudsley Family Research Studies team at the Institute of Psychiatry in London. She has authored several books and journal articles.

Contents

PART 1 A REVIEW OF THE LITERATURE ON SUPPORT FOR
ADOPTIONS IN DIFFICULTY

1. Introduction and method   3

The aims, focus and means of conducting the literature review   3
Terminology   5

2. The need for support, routine provision and user   7
feedback

Pre-placement adversities and post-placement adjustment   7
Separation, loss and maltreatment   7
The problems of looked after children and children placed   9
from care
Level of disturbance compared with children living with   10
their birth families
Problems and challenges as reported by new parents   10
Level of difficulty as perceived by parents   11
Stability over time of findings on the severity of problems   12
The new parents, family functioning and family integration   12
Summary   14
Calls for service expansion   14
Support from the social work service and health and   16
education services
Measuring satisfaction with services   19
Adopters' views on the social work service   20
The needs of minority ethnic adoptive families   23
Surveys of post-adoption service providers   23
Summary   24

3. The development of specialist services, interventions and evidence of effectiveness — 26

The development of post-adoption agencies — 26
Examples of pioneering agencies in the UK — 26
User-led organisations — 28
Developments elsewhere — 29
More specialised interventions — 31
A typology: from preventive approaches to more specific interventions — 32
Psychotherapy with the placed children — 33
Attachment-based interventions — 34
An example of child psychotherapeutic work — 36
More radical approaches — 38
Intervention with adoptive parents — 39
Intervention with the whole family — 41
Evidence of effectiveness — 44
Comments on evaluative studies — 44
Summary — 45

4. UK Government policy and current initiatives — 46

Recognition of the need — 46
Inspecting the quality of services — 47
Improving practice — 48
New legislation — 50
Summary — 52

PART 2   THE UK SURVEY

5. Context and method — 55

The context of the survey — 55
The aims of the survey — 56
Methods — 57
The sample — 58
The extent of participation by voluntary adoption agencies — 61
Who did we talk to? — 61
What did we ask about? — 63
Summary — 64

6. Agencies' responses to the challenge of improving practice   65

The profile of adoption within councils and in senior management   65
Funding issues   66
The profile of the agencies' adoption work   67
The profile of children placed for adoption April 2000–March 001   68
Changes in the profile of children placed for adoption   71
Summary   73
The level and type of need among adoptive families   74
The organisation of local authority children's and family placement services   75
Children's services   76
Family placement services   78
Post-adoption teams   78
Joint working between children's and families' social workers   79
Training in adoption work for children's social workers   81
Systems and procedures to improve communication   82
Voluntary adoption agencies   85
Summary   85

7. Current support services: routine and specialist   87

Who should provide support?   87
Service level agreements and purchasing arrangements   88
Pros and cons of contracting out   89
The family placement teams   90
Training for family placement or adoption workers   91
Adoption support services for adoptive families   93
Proactive, preventive services   93
Arrangements for managing contact and searching   96
Work with families in need after the order   97
Voluntary adoption agencies – provision of support   100
Other projects   100
Summary   104
Links across agencies and disciplines   106
The use and function of consortia   106
Education services   107
Therapeutic services for children and families   109

Joining up services   111
Crossing boundaries   113
Monitoring the views of users   114
Services for families of minority ethnicity   115
Burning issues   116
What we didn't ask about   116
Regional variations   117
Summary   117

8. Discussion and conclusions   120

Assessment of need and planning service provision   120
Delivery of adoption support services   122
Effectiveness   124
Conclusions   124

References   125

Part 1
A Review of the Literature on
Support for Adoptions in Difficulty

1 Introduction and method

Adoption is a means of providing stability and nurturance for some children who cannot live with their birth families. Children, who perhaps have had adequate parenting at some time in the past, or those who have shown remarkable resilience despite the difficulties they have faced, may progress very well in their new homes. Others may bring a host of problems with them that do not easily diminish, and indeed may persist or reappear over time and present a considerable challenge to the new parents. It is these adoptions that we are concerned with here. In the pages that follow we present a literature review of adoption support followed by a UK-wide survey of services provided by adoption agencies and their views on needs and current provisions. Neither the review nor the survey claims to provide totally comprehensive coverage of adoption support and we acknowledge that it leans more towards *late* adoptions from care and the psychological and social needs of the children and new families. We conclude with our thoughts on how these survey findings take us forward and on the need for further research.

The aims, focus and means of conducting the literature review

The five-year strategy (2002–07) of the British Agencies for Adoption and Fostering (BAAF, 2002) states that:

Children and carers need access to a range of services including education, health and other support to enable families to parent children separated from their family of origin.

In this review we aim to bring together as much of the published literature and other written materials as we can find that are relevant to post-placement and post-adoption support for adoptive families and to attempt a synthesis. For practical reasons we have had to restrict ourselves to articles written in English and we have also had to narrow our focus to make the task manageable. First, we focus purely on placements from local authority care into non-relative adoptive families. Second, we concentrate solely on services for the adoptive parents and their children and within that our interest is mainly on the services for adoptive families that are experiencing difficulties.

Many aspects of adoption support have therefore been excluded from the review. This does not mean to convey, however, that they are less important, nor that they should be accorded less significance in planning a comprehensive adoption service. For example, the need to respond to the needs of birth families, post-placement and post-adoption, is not considered here, although this has come to be seen increasingly as an important part of the service in its own right as well as having the potential to contribute to positive contact arrangements, and in turn, to the stability of the placement. Managing complex contact arrangements with birth parents, siblings and other key figures is an increasingly important practice development, but a full examination of this topic would divert from the main thrust of this review.

The needs of adults adopted as children, whether for psychological help or for counselling with regard to knowledge of their origins, were also not considered. Similarly, pre-placement preparation and information-giving about the children's history may well be crucial in influencing the placement but they are not the main focus. Financial assistance and practical services are not dealt with in detail, nor are meeting very specific educational and medical needs, nor post-disruption reviews and support. The special needs of kinship adoptions, transracial and international adoptions are not considered here in themselves, although much of what follows may still be highly relevant.

The central area of interest is, therefore, promoting the security of adoptive placements for children from public care. The main areas covered in this review are the relationship between pre-placement adversities and post-placement adjustment of the children; the challenges to the new parents; the development of services and users' perspectives; more specialised interventions for severe or enduring difficulties; the evaluation of effectiveness of interventions and the development of government policy.

This literature review will follow, as far as possible, current guidelines for conducting systematic reviews (Cooper, 1998) although from the outset it was recognised that, as this is an emerging subject, examples of empirical and evaluative research would be in the minority compared with practice papers, theoretical discussions, and reports of policy and service innovations. The following electronic databases were searched for journal articles between 1965 and the present: Psychinfo, Medline, Embase, Caredata, Childata and the Cochrane Library. The following key phrases were used to perform the search: Adoption and support; Adoption and services; Adoption and intervention; Adoption and post-placement; Adoption and post-adoption. Adoption websites were consulted in the UK (BAAF, Adoption UK, After Adoption, Coram Family, Post Adoption Centre) and in the USA (The Evan Donaldson Adoption Institute, Oregon Post Adoption Resource Centre (ORPARC); National Adoption Information Clearinghouse (NAIC)). UK government publications were searched via COIN and POINT and the Department of Health adoption website. In addition, bibliographies, reference lists attached to relevant articles and chapters, training manuals and agency documents were consulted. Furthermore, in seeking comments from experts in the field on the review, we also asked them to cite any important papers that might have been missed. About 120 references were located and reviewed.

The search for relevant papers was lengthy because the literature is very dispersed and not as easily retrievable electronically as topics in, say, medicine or psychology. Relevant papers appear in a range of journals including child psychiatry, individual, group and family therapy journals as well as in agency publications, child welfare policy and practice papers.

Terminology

Until very recently support for adoptive families and their children has been described or thought about in terms of *post-placement* and *post-adoption*. These have been perceived as two distinct phases. The significance is that the responsibilities of local authorities change substantially at the point of adoption. Statutory welfare supervision of children placed for adoption is a legal requirement (s33 of the Adoption Act 1976 in England and Wales) but following the adoption order, the local authority supervisory role terminates and legal rights and responsibilities are transferred in total to the new parents. However, the issues and concerns of the child and family do not take on a radically different form at the point of legalisation of the placement, so we need a term that covers forms of assistance that might be required at any time from preparation for the placement onwards. The term *post-placement* support will not suffice, as it is not appropriate to continue to refer to a legalised adoption as a placement. The term *post-adoption* is often inappropriate because a lengthy period of placement may occur before adoption takes place and it may imply that services are only to be provided after adoption. In line with the most recent consultation document to emerge from the Department of Health (2002), we shall employ the term *adoption support* when we mean to transcend the legal division.

2 The need for support, routine provision and user feedback

Pre-placement adversities and post-placement adjustment

We know, from a substantial body of research, that a significant minority of adoptive placements of looked after children either continue, but with enduring difficulties, or disrupt (Rushton *et al*, 2000; Triseliotis, 2002). We know too that the factors most strongly associated with difficult placements are older age at placement and the child's adverse experiences in previous environments. The primary reasons for difficulties are usually related to behavioural challenges presented by the children and problems in establishing satisfactory relationships between each of the members of the newly created family. Relationship difficulties may exist between parent and child or between related or unrelated children. It is important to stress that accumulating research findings show that placement outcomes are not usually determined by single events or risk factors but are the product of interactions. These include interactions between the child's experiences prior to placement; genetic and temperamental variables in the child; the child's present difficulties and strengths; the adoptive family's structure and coping capacities; and the extent and quality of informal and professional support provided.

Separation, loss and maltreatment

Children placed for adoption from care, except those placed from birth, will have experienced separation from attachment figures and will have lost significant relationships in their lives. Many will have experienced some form of maltreatment, whether intentioned or not. There is a growing literature on the antecedents and consequences of various types of maltreatment and neglect which adoption professionals and, indeed, adoptive families themselves need to be aware of in order to understand the child's post-placement adjustment. It has been shown that maltreatment affects development across a wide spectrum of psycho-social functioning. Comprehensive reviews by Skuse and Bentovim (1994), Cicchetti and Toth

(1995) summarise the known effects upon emotional, relationship, and cognitive problems, educational performance and behavioural difficulties. It has proved more of a challenge to establish whether the sub-types of maltreatment, that is, physical, emotional, sexual abuse and neglect have differential outcomes. On the whole, studies have not found much direct correspondence between events and effects. This is likely to be because abuse rarely falls into one category and the outcomes will be influenced by a range of factors including the intensity and duration of the maltreatment; combinations of types of adversity; other aspects of the birth family environment; the identity of the perpetrator or perpetrators of abuse; the vulnerability of the child; and the availability of supports. The links are therefore complex and result in a range of outcomes. Furthermore, the *meaning* of these pre-placement events for the child will influence outcome (Rutter, 1989). Future research will need to deal with these confounding factors when conducting follow-up studies into the consequences of the sub-types of abuse (MacMillan and Munn, 2001).

A tendency has been evident in the practice literature to emphasise the contribution of stresses and trauma on the children, but it is important not to ignore the influence of factors prior to any mistreatment like poor maternal nutrition or health during the pregnancy and pre-natal exposure to drug and alcohol misuse. Additionally, a higher risk exists of inherited mental health problems in children adopted from care because certain psychiatric problems and anti-social behaviour are more likely to be present in the birth parents. However, genetic factors do not affect the children's development directly but rather may make them vulnerable to or protect them from environmental influences (Rutter, 2000).

More recently, research has been conducted into neurological changes associated with pre-natal, neo-natal and childhood stress and maltreatment (Perry, 1995; Schore, 1996; Fisher, Gunnar, Chamberlain and Reid, 2000). Early adverse experiences may have lasting negative effects when they occur during sensitive periods in the development of the brain. Advances in the psychobiology of child maltreatment may prove increasingly important in explaining some common behavioural characteristics, for example, high activity levels, frequently found among looked after children, as well as aggressive responses and educational under achievement (see Glaser, 2000 for a comprehensive review). Although placement outcomes are inversely related to age at placement, infants can nevertheless be affected by the quality of care they received.

The problems of looked after children and children placed from care

Before the 1960s, little systematic enquiry had been conducted into the characteristics and problem profiles of children placed in different settings in the care system. Since then there has been an accumulation of evidence on the range and persistence of problems of children in residential care, foster care and adoption (Yule and Raynes, 1972; Rowe, Cain, Hundleby and Keane, 1984; Sinclair and Gibbs, 1998; Quinton and Rushton *et al*, 1998; Triseliotis, 2002). In the US, both Groze (1996) and Barth and Berry (1988) have shown that most children placed from care when older exhibited significant behavioural disturbances.

UK studies have mostly relied on standardised questionnaires to parents as a means of assessing the child's difficulties rather than independent observations of the children or of parent–child interaction. Other information has been gathered from teachers, independent professional assessments and, much less commonly, from the viewpoint of the placed children. Studies have mostly been cross-sectional, and based on data at one point in time, but are much more informative if samples can be followed up to establish whether difficulties disappear or whether placements that start out as largely problem-free become difficult later. Rushton, Mayes, Dance and Quinton (in press) have shown that over the first year in a late placed sample, child-to-parent relationship problems persisted, but only for a minority, while behavioural difficulties were both more common at the outset of the placement and more likely to persist than decrease.

Although follow-up studies have been conducted on infant adoptions (e.g. Fergusson, Lynskey and Horwood, 1995; Maughan, Collishaw and Pickles, 1998) no late placement samples in the UK have been followed prospectively beyond adolescence and so our knowledge of the adolescent adjustment of representative samples is still limited. However, retrospective research can still be informative. Howe's study (1997) showed that the combination of having a "poor start" in life and being placed late for adoption was associated with the worst outcome. Many of these children at adolescence were angry, hostile, confused and frustrated. However, much had improved for them by young adulthood. This illustrates the importance of appreciating adoption as a lifelong process.

Level of disturbance compared with children living with their birth families

If the first question is to ascertain what level and type of difficulty is present in these children, the second is to ask whether they are different, and how different, from children not separated from their birth parents (Peters, Atkins and McKay, 1999). Several outcome studies have used standardised measures and produced similar results. The Maudsley team, based in London, using Goodman's Strengths and Difficulties Questionnaires, found problem levels of the placed children, when at average age 14½ years, which was 5–6 years after placement, substantially elevated compared with matched community controls, both on total scores and all individual domains, especially over-activity, conduct and peer problems (Rushton and Dance, in preparation). Psychological problems had persisted for the group well into placement and 40 per cent scored in the abnormal range (17–40) versus 6 per cent for the controls. It is true that the controls, because they were volunteers, may have introduced selection bias. Careful measurement of the extent of continuing problems in representative samples constitutes some of the strongest evidence on which to build an argument for long-term support and intervention.

Problems and challenges as reported by new parents

In the attempt to record the placed children's problems, somewhat different responses are produced depending on the question that is asked. If adoptive parents are asked 'what troubles you most about the child?' different information may be produced compared with asking 'which of the following pre-selected problems does your child have?' In some ways, knowing which difficulties are producing the greatest strain for the parents is more useful when thinking about how to respond with relevant services. However, different types of difficulty head the list in different studies. Sometimes behavioural difficulties predominate and sometimes educational or financial problems. This may, of course, reflect differences in the samples of children placed. For example, health and information needs tend to predominate in samples containing many children with disabilities; cognitive problems in samples with children with pre-natal substance exposure and financial needs in lower-income families. Findings on problem frequencies are sometimes presented as if they generalised to all children placed for adoption.

It may be helpful to consider the following grouping of problems which children exhibit in the home setting in the first year of placement. This information is derived from research interviews with new parents in the two Maudsley studies of late placed children (5–11 years) (Quinton and Rushton *et al*, 1998; Rushton and Dance *et al*, 2001).

Level of difficulty as perceived by parents

1. *Common but manageable problems* – emotional distress, anxiety, sleeping difficulties, incontinence and mild eating problems.
2. *Problems presenting a stronger parenting challenge* – conduct problems, defiance, un-co-operativeness, stealing, lying, over-activity, restlessness, poor attention, sexualised behaviour. These behaviours have more of a negative impact on family life and relationships and are likely to need more carefully worked out parenting strategies and skills to manage them effectively.
3. *Problems that are a threat to placement stability* in that they stretch, or are beyond, the coping ability of the adoptive parents, severe parent–child relationship problems, weak return of affection or rejection, extreme forms of behaviour, especially persistent non-compliance, violence and aggression. These are more likely to challenge parents to the point of questioning the wisdom of the placement and more specific and sustained supportive interventions will be needed.

These are general categories and, of course, particular problems are more troublesome to some parents than others because of their own personalities, values and tolerance levels. For example, sexualised behaviour or academic difficulties may have much more impact on certain parents.

It is important to recognise that problems should not be thought of solely in individual terms or only as parent–child problems. Difficult interactions may arise between children placed as a sibling group and between placed children and children already in the family. Sibling disputes, rivalries and jealousies can be severe and unrelenting and a major challenge to adoptive parents. Managing these relationships may require expert help and the employment of specifically designed interventions (Rushton and Dance *et al*, 2001).

Stability over time of findings on the severity of problems

Reference to any studies on the level of children's disturbed behaviour will need to be made in the light of changes over time in the characteristics of the "in care" population, changes in the types of risk that children are exposed to, and changes in child welfare practice and service levels. Any policies which reduce maltreatment and delays in decision-making and improve case planning for separated children may reduce the level of pathology among the children. On the other hand, if inadequate resources and quality of training give rise to superficial assessments, poor matches, rushed adoptions and ineffective post-placement support, this may increase the level of psycho-social problems and the risk of poor placement outcome. It will be necessary to monitor developments in child welfare practice, to be aware of the changing profiles of the placed children and to gather feedback from the families to make sure that current needs are accurately identified and the response is flexibly attuned to them.

The new parents, family functioning and family integration

Researchers are beginning to investigate the significance of the role played by the new parents in promoting successful placements. Many suggestions are made in the practice literature on what the likely positive characteristics might be, for example being child-oriented, and having realistic expectations, a flexible parenting style, sound motivation and supportive partners. Indeed, it is likely that, due to their motivation to adopt and to the selection process, most adoptive families have above average capacities. Erich and Leung (1998) have made one of the few attempts to measure adoptive family life. They gave family functioning questionnaires to parents in long-term intact adoptions. Most of the families were found to have good family functioning: that is, they were high on problem solving, communication skills, cohesiveness and future orientation. Cohen and Coyne *et al* (1993) found that adoptive families seeking help had greater psycho-social resources and better family functioning than non-adoption clinic referrals and she recommended that these strengths could be relied upon more in devising therapeutic interventions.

Some evidence is emerging about the contribution of carer charac-teristics in the formation of attachments in non-related infant–parent relationships. Dozier and Chase Stovall *et al* (2001) studied 50 pairs of foster mothers and their foster children. The mothers were given the Adult Attachment Interview (AAI) (George and Kaplan *et al*, 1996) and the children participated in the Strange Situation (Ainsworth and Blehar *et al*, 1978). About half the mothers were coded as having an autonomous state of mind. Most of the children had been abused and/or neglected and about half the children were classified as insecure. A 72 per cent concord-ance rate was found between the foster mother's state of mind and the infant's attachment, that is, autonomous mothers were more likely to have secure infants. It was also striking that so many had formed secure attachments, at least in the short term.

It is important to recognise, however, when assessing the capacities of prospective adopters, that certain characteristics that may be apparent at recruitment interviews, like warmth and sensitive parenting, may not be easy to maintain in the face of later severe difficulties. For example, parents may be unable to sustain their positive feelings in the face of an unresponsive, rejecting or poorly attached child (Dance, Rushton and Quinton, 2002).

An important development is the recognition of a need for a longer-term perspective on adoption; not simply during the early stages of placement but throughout childhood and adolescence and even beyond. For example, Pinderhughes and Rosenberg (1990) have developed an understanding of family readjustment in relation to late placed children. They are interested in how the families adjust and re-adjust in reaction to new developmental hurdles in the children. They recognise that a new member or members can destabilise the system, which has to go through a restabilising process. They argue that, if these phases are regarded as expected, this may improve acceptance and tolerance of difficult behaviour.

This more recent focus on family functioning is important for the development of support services. Knowledge currently being developed on family strengths as well as difficulties is crucial for crafting a well attuned service response, and employing a model of family development over time is very valuable for considering how to expand a support service beyond the early phase of placement.

Summary

- Children placed from care beyond infancy are likely to have multiple problems.
- The problems will be many times more common than in the non-separated population.
- For some children, problems will be persistent and so a longer-term view is necessary.
- Behavioural problems are more common than parent–child relationship problems.
- Early adverse experiences may affect the process of brain development.
- Weak return of affection or rejection, and persistent non-compliance, violence and aggression are the most challenging behaviours for adoptive parents.
- Systematic collection of evidence is important in order to assist placements in difficulty.
- Complex patterns of adjustment and re-adjustment will occur in the children and the adoptive family over time.
- Services need to be flexible to match the changing profile of children in adoptive placements.

Calls for service expansion

As mentioned earlier, until very recently the post-placement but pre-order and the post-order phases of adoption have been viewed as quite separate because of the change in legal status and transfer of responsibility that the adoption order confers. However, families and practitioners will attest to the fact that little else is likely to change dramatically just because an adoption certificate has been issued. Some issues such as educational needs are likely to be ongoing and other concerns are likely to arise as children reach different stages of development. Traditionally, adoptive parents and their children have had to gain access to mainstream services if problems have emerged after adoption. The notion of a comprehensive post-adoption service has grown only gradually, often through the pioneering work of voluntary agencies, initially in the US but later replicated and further developed in the UK. This is not only a recognition of the presence of both ongoing and late emerging problems, but also a reflection of the increasing complexity of adoptive placements and the demands made on adoptive families regardless of whether there are difficulties with the adoptive placement itself.

With the emergence of the permanency principle (Maluccio, Fein and Olmstead, 1986), and as more "special needs" children were being placed with families during the 1970s and 1980s, increasing recognition was given to the extent of unmet need and calls for support for new families began to grow. The topic began to receive more attention in the UK from the 1980s onwards (Macaskill, 1985; Macaskill, 1986; Phillips, 1988; Rushton, 1989; Borland et al, 1991a, b; Rushton et al, 1993; Logan and Hughes, 1995; Yates, 1995; Triseliotis et al, 1997; Hill and Shaw, 1998; Mather, 2001). Much of this adoption literature has been concerned to point out various shortcomings in support services and to encourage a more active and tailored response to the needs. The voice of adopters of special needs children is often reported in these articles and studies complaining that professionals have not understood the extent of problems in the adopted children, have not taken their concerns seriously or have made inappropriate recommendations for resolving problems.

Indeed, it is now 15 years since Argent (1987) brought together writings from a series of individuals with a professional or personal involvement in adoption, especially special needs adoption, to explore the level of need and potential modes of response.

Many of the appeals for better services since this time have come from social workers or therapists who have found themselves involved with families who were struggling to make a placement or an adoption work (e.g. Mulcahy, 1999). Others have come from researchers who have discovered high levels of unmet need in the course of their contact with adoptive families. Although adoptive families in the early years often did not feel they had the right to demand services or were reluctant to admit they needed help, gradually there has been a more realistic assessment of the challenges involved and a greater formal acknowledgement of need. Indeed, over time adopters themselves have become more vocal and have drawn strength from hearing of each other's experience of parenting and of seeking help.

The view was becoming more forcefully expressed that there was not only a need to provide support to adoptive parents after the child was placed, but also a need for adequate access to services beyond the point of adoption. Many questions then arise as to what support means in this context, who should provide it, and who should pay for it. To begin with, support for adoptive parents appeared to be required in a variety of forms, commonly categorised as financial, emotional and practical. However, it was difficult to think in terms of a standard package given that people's expectations and experience of support will vary, depending on their level of need and their own personal resources.

Support from the social work service and health and education services

The first port of call for adoptive families in the UK, particularly prior to the adoption order being granted, will be the agency or agencies that arranged the placement. The agency responsible for placing a child in the UK will almost always be a local authority. The agency responsible for the recruitment and preparation of the family may be a local authority or a voluntary adoption agency. Typically a placement will be made and then supervised by a children's social worker (CSW) based in the local authority, and a family social worker (FSW) from the family placement team or adoption agency will also remain involved.[1]

---

[1] A word about terminology. Titles for the departments and agencies responsible for adoption practice in the UK vary across the four countries, for example, in England social services departments (SSDs) hold statutory responsibility for looked after children, while in Scotland this falls to social work departments. Job titles for managers and practitioners likewise differ between agencies. We shall try to be consistent here and refer to SSDs to indicate *all* local authority agencies, VAAs to represent all voluntary adoption agencies, FSW for the family's social worker (whether from an SSD or VAA) and CSW for the children's social worker.

Once the child has been placed with a new family with a plan for adoption, the front line work to support the placement will usually be supplied jointly by the child's social worker and the family social worker. Since at least the late 1980s, there has been a practice in the UK of providing regular and occasionally intensive social work support to most adoptive placements at least up until the point of the adoption order being made (Rushton, 1989; Quinton and Rushton *et al*, 1998). Although several agencies have maintained an "open door" approach to adopters after the order, until recently it has been common for routine contact and support, from both workers (CSW and FSW), to cease at the point of adoption. However, research has shown that these roles were exercised by two contrasting groups of staff (Rushton, 2000). The FSWs were likely to have more time to spend on each case, mostly directed their attention towards the new parents, and had a more specialist and focused role compared with CSWs who also were juggling with the competing demands of child protection responsibilities.

Continuing services provided by local authority social workers have varied according to the understanding and the priorities of individual practitioners and departmental managers. Any developments before 1998/9 will have been achieved without additional funding. Voluntary adoption agencies have long had a reputation for being more proactive post adoption order, often keeping in touch with adopters and children long after an order has been granted by means of regular social events and activities.

Recognition has grown in special needs adoption that help may be needed in talking to children and young people about their early lives, or with seeking out birth family members, or with managing contact arrangements with the birth family (Mackaskill, 2002; Neil, 2002). These aspects of support should be part of standard service provision for adoptive families (Department of Health, 2001). However, in the early days of service development, the focus was on behavioural difficulties and helping children to settle and become a part of the family, as some families were found to be struggling with serious problems that threatened the placement. The literature on how best to support adoptive families started to expand in the US following the initiatives to place special needs children. The writings of Fahlberg (1994) and Jewett (1995) were highly

17

influential and their ideas were embraced by individual practitioners and managers in the UK and were largely responsible for moving both voluntary agencies and SSDs forward in thinking about adoption services. However, the clinic-based, psychoanalytically oriented child psychotherapy world from which these ideas emanated could often be difficult to transfer to the greatly different culture of the services normally provided by the UK education, health and social services. Nevertheless, the ideas and theoretical underpinnings of these writers have informed adoption practice in the UK. We shall go on to look at some of the developments that have grown from this, mostly in the voluntary sector, later in the text.

In sum, it was becoming clear that the needs of adoptive families were multi-faceted, some needing help in securing appropriate educational or health services, others needing assistance with management of behaviour problems or over-activity, and still others needing guidance in building meaningful relationships with their children. Such a variety of problems, it was becoming recognised, could not always be effectively addressed by a family's social worker and the involvement of the combined expertise of a multi-disciplinary team was often needed.

Until quite recently the majority of families needing help beyond what a social worker could provide have had to seek help from universal services. For the most part, this would be local Child and Adolescent Mental Health Services (CAMHS). In adoptive families, unlike families with children in need, the service needs of the children and the parents are rather different. The CAMH service may be appropriate for the child, but perhaps not for the parents where the need is to build on existing family strengths and experiences rather than to seek to explain how they might be implicated in the problem. Adoptive families are for the most part healthy and well motivated and want a partnership with professionals to help them deal more effectively with special parenting difficulties and challenges. Innovation Projects are being set up to improve the mental health of children and young people and to improve links between CAMHS and other services (Kurtz, 2001). The nature of CAMH services is likely to change in the future and it will be important to learn whether CAMHS generally are making appropriate modifications to provide a more appropriate service to adoptive families.

Although the crucial role of education of children in the care system is increasingly recognised (Jackson, 2001), the appropriateness and effectiveness of educational provision for children adopted from care is worthy of further investigation. In an early study of late placements (Rushton, Treseder and Quinton, 1988) it was reported that school and school problems assumed larger importance as the placement progressed. Parents had to adjust to slow educational progress and to respond to the school's reports of difficult behaviour, poor relationships with peers and teachers, and communication and concentration problems. Parents have continued to have battles with the education system about obtaining psychological assessments, appropriate school placements and educational help and advice. The school system, like the therapeutic system, also needs to be more adoption-sensitive.

Measuring satisfaction with services

In recent years there has been increasing interest in surveying the opinions of users of services in order to incorporate their views into shaping and improving future provision of adoption support services. But questions remain about how accurate and how valid are the data gathered so far. How well represented has the adopters' experience been? Is the complexity of users' views being captured? What is the level of agreement on what is needed between providers and users?

Edwards and Staniszewska (2000), in their review of research into the user's perspective, complain that consumer research usually lacks a theoretical foundation so that it is not at all clear what the term "satisfaction" means. Satisfaction can have many facets and there is a danger of reductionism. Brief and quickly completed satisfaction questionnaires sent out by adoption agencies may be constrained by the question posed rather than encouraging respondents to say whatever they think, and little opportunity is given to qualify responses.

A variety of means of assessment has been used by different agencies and different studies have produced widely differing overall satisfaction levels. Clearly this disparity may depend on what sort of placement is being evaluated, and the differently phrased research questions. Furthermore, if new parents do not know their entitlement and what might be available, it is not easy for them to say if they are or are not satisfied. Edwards and Staniszewska (2000) argue that qualitative research using group discussions is likely to produce more consideration of and reflection on services. The existing research on "satisfaction" is therefore rather soft, so that it has been difficult to reach general conclusions. Research into adopters' views tends to stand outside the considerable literature on service satisfaction and efforts need to be made to manage the difficulties in measuring satisfaction meaningfully. It would be useful, as a start, for researchers to work towards agreement on what standard items should be included under the concept of service satisfaction.

Adopters' views on the social work service

Information on the views of adopters comes from a number of sources. No large-scale representative UK-wide survey of adopters' opinions on services exists as yet although there are several research studies, rather than agency-based enquiries, that have examined support services. We have one major national study (based in England and Wales) focusing on post-adoption support conducted in 1994 (Lowe and Murch *et al*, 1999). This was a three-part study: a family study, an adopted children study and an agency study. The agency study will be referred to later on.

The family study was concerned with children late placed (at five years and older). Unfortunately, as with many such studies, the authors received only a 40 per cent response rate to postal questionnaires, which may be average for this means of inquiry, but they were still missing 60 per cent of the responses. Many research respondents were lost because of disrupted placements, which inevitably skewed the provision of information. Although the authors found some examples of well-supported placements, in general the families made it clear that services were hard to come by and concluded that: 'good quality adoption services were a lottery'.

The authors are appropriately cautious in not claiming positive outcomes for services without sufficient data but they say that, 'adoption support can sometimes make the difference between a placement succeeding or disrupting'. They recommended standard levels of eligibility and of financial support and that legislation should be changed from an obligation to an "express duty" to provide services and that more precise expectations of services were needed.

The views of adopted children on the support or services they need have rarely been sought and is a major gap in the literature. The Thomas and Beckford *et al* study (1999), *Adopted Children Speaking*, was a bold attempt to elicit the views of adopted children although the children often found it hard to remember what their social workers had offered when asked to recall some time later.

Phillips' study (1988) was based on interviews with 19 adoptive families in two regions in Scotland. The children had been in placement up to five years and were average age 11. Problems experienced by families were found to be both wide-ranging and long-lived. The new parents had low expectations of post-placement support and they reported that visits stopped abruptly after the adoption order. They were largely unaware of other services apart from whatever the placing agency provided. It is important to note, however, that the majority of adopters did not want the visits to continue as they thought it might upset the child or because they valued their independence.

The Maudsley studies (Rushton and Quinton *et al*, 1993; Rushton *et al*, 1995; Quinton and Rushton *et al*, 1998; Rushton, 1999) have revealed a fairly consistent picture of regular and sometimes intensive social work visiting in the first year of placement, although this was mostly withdrawn after adoption. The encouragement and affirmation of the adopters' parenting skill was welcome, as were attempts to explain the child's difficult or odd behaviour, but little practical parenting advice was received. For example, lying and stealing were very prominent in the placed children and this behaviour posed difficulties for most carers who wanted to be offered specific techniques and strategies. The service satisfaction varied with the skill and expertise of individual practitioners and ease of access to specialist services. Parents often said they had difficulty seeking help because of a fear of failure and an expectation that they should cope alone. They feared being blamed for the difficulties and that disclosure of their shortcomings or feelings of being overwhelmed may lead to the possibility of removal of the child by the local authority.

At the five-year follow-up on the first study, none of the families was receiving a local authority service and referrals for specialist help had not resulted in any substantial engagement with relevant services. By the eight-year follow-up, psychological, psychiatric and educational help had been sought independently by some of the parents. The authors concluded: 'It is imperative that post-placement and post-adoption counselling is provided to all who need it by trained and properly supervised staff with recent access to research based knowledge.'

Thoburn and Murdoch *et al* (1986) investigated 15 families with special needs children placed by the Children's Society in Norwich. In relation to the family social workers from the project, the new parents wanted not a prescriptive but a consultative approach whereby they would be given the opportunity to explore alternative ways of handling problems. A show of genuine concern for the families was seen as the most important factor in determining whether the service was helpful.

A number of user satisfaction surveys have been conducted in the US (e.g. Marcenko and Smith, 1991; Rosenthal and Groze *et al*, 1996) although they will not be reported here as we are not in a position to know the quality of mainstream services and the ease of access to supports. Satisfaction levels without this contextual information can be meaningless. However, from a methods point of view, a recent study by McDonald and Propp *et al* (2001) is worth consulting as an example of a rigorous quantitative approach designed to elicit more detailed feedback on the numerous components of a modernised service and to examine predictors of post-placement adjustment. They followed up families from an agency in Kansas two years after placement; the children had on average been 7½ years old at placement. Thirteen statements about the adoption process were provided to rate for satisfaction and a lengthy checklist was presented of services needed and services used. Not all families wanted all services. The majority (90 per cent) of those who replied said they had received the services they wanted although, as there was no independent evaluation, we do not know with what effect. The need for support groups, respite care and a child psychotherapist service was frequently not met.

Nearly half the families did not reply to the questionnaires despite strenuous efforts by the researchers. This flags up a general difficulty in eliciting feedback as many families will be reluctant to maintain any agency contact. However, this is one of the few studies to compare respondent and non-respondent characteristics to check for bias in the findings. In fact, the non-respondent families had children with more special needs and the absence of their views in the survey may have skewed the findings in a more positive direction.

The needs of minority ethnic adoptive families

Despite the special efforts that are being made to recruit adopters whose racial and cultural backgrounds are matched to those of black and mixed heritage children, little research material is available on the particular needs of black and Asian and other minority ethnic adoptive families. It is important to know whether these families are satisfied with the quality and sensitivity of adoption support: in particular, do the families feel that racial stereotyping or discrimination was at work or did they think a culturally competent service was being offered. These questions need to be asked of health, housing, educational and financial support services as well as the social work services. A practice literature is growing on help for the children which includes: promoting a positive sense of racial identity in children (Banks, 1992a, b); the significance of black sibling relationships (Prevatt-Goldstein and Spencer, 2000); and the placement progress of black adopted children (Thoburn and Norford et al, 2000). The Post Adoption Centre in London is one agency which has begun to offer workshops for carers of black children.

Surveys of post-adoption service providers

Only one large-scale study of adoption agencies has so far been conducted in the UK. Lowe and Murch et al (1999) obtained data from questionnaires in 1994 from 115 agencies (44 voluntary, 71 statutory: a 72 per cent response rate). A representative sample of agencies (n = 45) was then selected for research interviews to elicit more detailed responses. The survey covered a wide range of adoption issues, only a small number of which were concerned with post-adoption support. Most of the respondents thought that staff time, resources, training and funding were inadequate to expand the service as they wished and thought necessary. Funding for specialist psychological services was hard to find and they commented specifically on the lack of training and support for staff working with minority families. Weak managerial support was held responsible for this state of under-development. By contrast, the authors found encouraging the development of strong links between statutory and voluntary agencies by way of formal service agreements.

A US-based study by McRoy (1999) sought the views of service providers by means of telephone interviews with 12 therapeutic agencies concerned with special needs adoptive families. The study concentrated on how practitioners theorised about the origin of the families' problems. The therapists saw the children as having unique difficulties due to their early experiences and regarded the capacity to bond with new parents as strongly related to successful placement. They saw one of their tasks as helping the family to come to terms with mis-placed expectations. They understood the children's feelings of sadness and anger as a result of loss, separation and abuse and thought that these feelings were projected onto the adopters because they were available. The children's counter-productive behaviours were seen as a means of coping with a new environment. A range of interventions was being used both to help the child achieve the aim of re-connecting with the past and to promote better family relations.

Summary

- Seen from the perspective of the adopters, routine social work support *post-placement* but *pre-adoption* has generally been well received, at least when concerned with positive encouragement and help to understand the child's problems.
- Service satisfaction, however, varies with the skill and expertise of individual practitioners.
- Sound advice on practical management of the children's difficulties has been lacking.
- Adoption support has been inadequately provided and unevenly spread.
- It has been hard to gain access to specialist psychological services and respite care.
- Those who received the services they requested have generally been satisfied.
- Opinions gathered about services need to be more than simple positive and negative responses and these opinions may emerge and vary over time.
- Less is known about those who choose not to seek services, who do

not follow up on referrals for services, or who quickly drop out of services offered. User research needs to be designed so that basic data are available on all the potential respondents in order to check for potential bias in responses.

- The consumer research is largely descriptive and lacking an examination of how levels of satisfaction and dissatisfaction with services relate to the type of support provided and to the characteristics of the children and the families.
- Very little is known about the views of children who receive post-placement support.
- Little is known about how cultural and ethnic variations in adoptive families relate to service satisfaction.

3 The development of specialist services, interventions and evidence of effectiveness

The development of post-adoption agencies

Examples of pioneering agencies in the UK

In the 1980s, services began to be created to fill in the gaps in exiting provision. Sawbridge (1990) has given an account of the Post Adoption Centre (PAC), the first of its kind in the UK, which opened in north London in 1986. By this time a considerable amount had been learnt about the support needs of adoptive families and although several voluntary and some local authority adoption agencies were developing their own post adoption service, this was not generally available throughout the UK. The PAC therefore aimed to offer a service to anyone involved in adoption regardless of area of residence or which agency had arranged the placement. The Centre consisted of a small staff of part-time counsellors. They were responding to adoptive families in need of support to begin with, but soon broadened their service to encompass the concerns of all the parties to adoption. Some issues have changed with changing populations and policies (e.g. "telling" and transracial adoptions) but they were already concerned with managing challenging behaviour in children, especially problems that were emerging in the teenage years. They were also beginning to apply a range of more specific interventions like behavioural techniques, individual counselling, group work and family therapy.

This new venture provided the first opportunity in the UK to seek the views of the service recipients. Howe (1990a) examined the referrals, and showed that a much longer time frame was needed to understand post-adoption adjustment. Howe (1990b) subsequently conducted a consumer feedback evaluation of the centre's services. Postal questionnaires were sent to 164 people who had received counselling at the centre in the first three years of operation. The response rate was 77 per cent. Of these, a very high level of satisfaction was expressed (91 per cent satisfied or very satisfied). The adopters expressed a wish for guidance on how to handle their children and their difficulties. They also needed a chance to talk and to express strong feelings of guilt, failure, anger and desperation and they needed appreciation of what it is like to be an adoptive parent.

It was clear that a need for specialist help had been identified and some users were beginning to articulate a wish for services to be provided independently from the SSD, from CAMHS and from placing agencies. Subsequently, Burnell and Briggs (1997a, b) described a project to set up a local base in East Sussex using the specialist knowledge they had developed at the PAC.

At the time that services were being developed to support adoptive parenting, so was the adoptive task becoming more complex. Contact arrangements with birth families were becoming more common and were placing an additional demand on post-placement services for support work and mediation. Preparation of all the parties for reunion, for continuing contact, and for post-contact review became a new challenge. New services were being called for but with no strategy for covering the additional cost. Reports began to appear in the literature on specially set up local services, for example, in Essex (Cunningham and Cohen, 1985), Hampshire (Magee and Thoday, 1995) and Norfolk (Beek, 1999). Workshops and post-adoption support groups began to be set up to help families to understand the possible origins of problems. Adopters seemed to benefit from attempts to understand the source of problems although, in relation to the earlier section on problem profiles, the origin, or origins, of this wide range of problems may not always be certain.

Other agencies, like Parents for Children, the Children's Society and Coram Family began to appoint post-adoption workers who could retain regular contact and provide support if required. After Adoption was set up in Manchester and Leeds and later in Wales; it also established Talk Adoption, a national freephone helpline for young people with any connection to adoption. The Keys Attachment Centre was established in Lancashire and Family Futures in London. However, developments were more in evidence in England than in Wales and Northern Ireland, although Watson and McGhee (1995) have reported on developing post-placement support in Scotland.

McGhee (1995) described a one-off consultancy service in Scotland.

The evaluation of the service was based on a pre- and post-consultation questionnaire (n = 27) and semi-structured interviews. The placed children had the common range of psycho-social problems and the families had felt a sense of abandonment by the services, which were under strain. Of those who received services, two-thirds reported that they had their expectations met. For some, fresh perspectives led to a change of parental response and a consequent reduction in problems. The respondents said they benefited from greater understanding, and from advice directed at parental action. A minority thought that little had changed or been offered to them as parents. A one-off session may have been too limited and too late for these families.

Many of these dedicated post-adoption agencies have not written up their approach in professional journals and so do not have a large presence in a literature review but the rationale and content of their service can be found in their publicity and websites. However, not enough information is normally supplied to know about the quality and effectiveness of the service or to be able to compare which approach might suit a family better. They often tend to stress the challenge presented by poorly attached children or imply that attachment difficulties are at the root of all the child's difficulties. The unsuspecting adopter may come to assume that "attachment explains all" when there might be other unexplored origins of the problem and well-tested interventions to target the problem directly may be available. A pressing need is evident for an exercise to compare and contrast and assess the contribution and effectiveness of the newer agencies.

Also of note has been the setting up of special clinics and Child and Family Departments in hospitals. Three London-based centres, the Tavistock Centre, Great Ormond Street Hospital and the Maudsley Hospital, have all developed services for adoptive families, have trained staff in specific interventions and are beginning to set up or to plan evaluations of their work.

User-led organisations

A significant development was the arrival of user-led organisations, beginning with the setting up in 1971 of the Parent to Parent Information on Adoption Services (PPIAS) by a group of adoptive parents. In 1999 the name was changed to Adoption UK but still with the aim of providing a self-help network offering local support groups and training workshops and resource and information packs. Their parent support programme called *It's a piece of cake?* is described more fully later on under the heading of parenting intervention. NORCAP (The National Organisation for Counselling Adoptees and Parents) was set up to assist adopted children, birth parents and adopters and has recently produced an offshoot called Rejection Network to help adopted people rejected by their birth parents.

Notable developments of a similar kind have taken place in the US. For example, the Oregon Post Adoption Resource Centre (ORPARC) offers a free service to Oregon adopters including a website with a newsletter, listings of existing support groups, teleconference training and advice on how to set up new groups. The organisation involves professionals but is mostly adopter-led.

Developments elsewhere

We are only beginning to obtain an international perspective on adoption and adoption services, although two recent studies (Selwyn and Sturgess, 2001; Warman and Roberts, 2002) are leading the way. It is clear that, in terms of within-country adoptions from care, the greatest numbers being placed are within the US and UK. Other countries use the route of non-relative adoption far less to achieve permanence and very little literature is available to refer to. The permanence movement and attempts to place special needs children in families began somewhat earlier in the US and more extensive developments have been taking place over a longer period. There were already 250 parent self-help groups in existence in 1980 (Meezan, 1980) and "buddy systems", and the number of helplines and information exchanges have grown. The National Resources Center for Special Needs Adoption was set up as early as 1985 by Spaulding for Children, and the Evan B Donaldson Adoption Institute was set up in 1996 to improve adoption policy and practice. A summary of important US initiatives in the 1990s can be found in a recent article by Barth and Miller (2000).

One early need, the sharing of useful information between adopters, began to be met with the advent of the internet. Such information can be very valuable if reliable and up-to-date. However, evidence on topics such as the psychological development of adopted children and post-adoption interventions can often be out of date, having been written over ten years ago when the organisations were first funded. The US view of child development can also be more psychoanalytically oriented than in the UK. References to Oedipal and Electra conflicts in adopted children tend to appear more frequently and are not so culturally acceptable in the UK.

A major feature of child welfare policy in the US has been the tension between policies to preserve families and to place children at risk away from home, especially via adoption (Pecora and Whittaker *et al*, 2000). The enthusiasm for family preservation interventions (see Family Preservation and Support Services Act, 1993) waned somewhat when initial results were not sufficiently impressive and the numbers in public care were large and growing. President Clinton's Initiative 2002 was a significant step as it required every state to double the number of adoptions out of care by 2002. Certain States, namely Illinois, Iowa, Oregon and Washington, are notable for promoting new developments and many more children are being placed as a result. Under the Adoption and Safe Families Act (ASFA, 1997), States are expected to fund a number of family services including post-adoption support. The US is therefore much closer to having an established funding base for post-adoption services.

Although based on US experience, the fullest account of thinking about adoption services occurs in the book by Smith and Howard called *Promoting Successful Adoptions: Practice with troubled families* (Smith and Howard, 1999). This is probably the most comprehensive and up-to-date book on therapeutic services, although the authors have yet to produce outcome data. The book is more a review of current knowledge, an outline of the principles of adoption preservation services and a distillation of the work of the Illinois Adoption Preservation Project (IAPP). The report of their work was not based on a representative sample of adoptions but a study of placements in difficulty referred in the early 1990s. The cases were an inclusive group of stranger, foster carer and relative adoptions. The principles on which the intervention services are built are given as being family-centred, ecological, and taking a developmental perspective and a strengths-based approach. The authors speculate on the function of conduct problems in adopted children and on unravelling inter-relationships between the child's feelings and behaviour. The service emphasises the need for adoptive parents to be helped to understand the effects of maltreatment on their child.

Although US services may be better developed than in the UK, similar problems have been faced in terms of inadequate resources and uncertainty about secure funding, unevenness in the geographical spread of provision of service, lack of knowledge and even insensitivity by mental health professionals to issues specific to adoptive families, lack of services for families with adopted adolescents and very little progress in developing secure knowledge on what works to support placements.

Efforts are currently being made in the US to apply the knowledge and experience gained in family preservation services, originally designed to prevent admission into care, by modifying these intensive home-based programmes to help adoptive families in crisis (Smith and Howard, 1999). Providing financial and other support for minority families has been crucial for the placement of minority ethnic children who are over-represented in children waiting for adoptive placements.

More specialised interventions

Over time, support services and interventions have developed in response to dissemination of the research findings and revelations of the short-comings of existing services. In trying to describe current services we are trying to catch a moving target since development is a continuing process. Previous sections have dealt with the more generalised services, which would probably fit into the "preventive" heading of the typology given below. In this section we deal with more specialised, individually focused, sometimes therapeutic, interventions that have been developed to assist placements and adoptions in difficulty. We suggest a typology of services to help in clarifying the service levels, grouping the range of relevant interventions according to a progression from preventive, through more problem-focused approaches, to individualised therapeutic services.

A typology: from preventive approaches to more specific interventions

Preventive
Helplines;
Linking or mentoring with other adopters;
Networks;
Newsletters;
Self-help;
Information giving;
Ongoing mutual support groups;
Advocacy.

More problem-focused
Specific education or skills-based intervention;
Multi-disciplinary consultancy service;
Direct work with parents – parenting skills training, advice and guidance;
Support groups for placed/adopted children;
Support in managing complex contact arrangements.

Clinical/therapeutic services
Crisis intervention;
Counselling;
Child psychotherapy;
Art therapy/drama therapy/play therapy with children;
Attachment-based interventions;
Cognitive-behavioural interventions;
Whole-family-based interventions – including birth children;
Couple therapy;
Group-based intervention;
Pharmacological intervention with individual children;
Residential care/respite care/hospitalisation.

It has become clearer over time that many special needs placements work remarkably well, but some families struggle on with a range of enduring difficulties and a minority have severe problems that on occasion are too severe for the placement to continue. We focus here on therapeutic interventions for placements in difficulty, as this is one of the more contentious areas of adoptive placement policy and practice. The volume of secure, research-based knowledge in this field remains very small. Interventions of proven effectiveness need urgently to be identified and employed in order to help to stabilise at-risk placements and to reduce the risk of disruption.

Practitioners need to consider which aspects of the new family to address in trying to achieve change. Some favour child-focused work, others prefer efforts to enhance parenting or support the couple, and others advocate total family involvement. Well-resourced multi-disciplinary teams may be able to offer a combination of selected interventions. Justifications for a particular approach are often to be found, whereas worked-through examples showing how the approach is delivered are somewhat harder to come by, and independent evaluations of the effectiveness of the interventions are extremely rare. It is as well to be somewhat wary of over-confident claims from practitioners and therapists in the absence of rigorous evaluation. The following review of interventions focuses on direct interventions with the placed children, intervention with the adoptive parents, intervention with the whole family, and concludes with a presentation of currently available effectiveness studies.

Psychotherapy with the placed children

It is hoped that the new family will, in offering stability and consistent nurturing, be the major influence on restoring the child to psychological health, but in those instances where this is not happening, or not happening swiftly enough, the question becomes whether psychotherapy can expedite the process of resolving the negative consequences of early adversity. As mentioned earlier, psychotherapeutic help for placed children has been a rare resource and the literature on therapeutic interventions specifically with children in adoptive placements is not very extensive. However, Boston and Szur's (1983) text on treating very disturbed children in the care system and Hodges' (1984) paper on adopted children in psycho-analytic treatment have been very influential.

More conventional approaches to working directly with the child concentrate on helping children to understand their past and present and offer the opportunity of discussing the meaning of adoption and other concerns independently of their current family. This may involve further work on life story books to fill in gaps and re-visiting what they had previously understood in the light of their developing understanding. For example, "Theraplay" has been developed as a means of helping children address past losses (Jernberg, 1993).

Adolescents in particular may benefit from individual counselling or psychotherapy when they have issues to resolve about their origins and experiences, identity or developing sexuality (Yeo, 1996). Therapeutic and support groups for adopted children are sometimes referred to as a useful resource in the literature although detailed accounts of interventions and outcomes are rare (but see Cordell and Nathan et al, 1985).

Attachment-based interventions

Great interest has been shown recently in applying attachment theory to the field of childcare in general and adoption in particular (Rutter and O'Connor, 1999). Although the bulk of the work remains concerned with early infant and birth parent relationships, the theory is being rapidly expanded to encompass the creation of new emotional bonds with strangers, as in late placement adoption, following insecure or broken attachments to key people prior to placement. Questions arise as to how an attachment is formed at this later stage and how far it might come to resemble a secure unbroken attachment made in infancy. Might the re-attachment process take place rapidly for some children, or take many years, or has this capacity perhaps been seriously compromised so that problems continue into adult life and relationships? Furthermore, do certain parent characteristics, family environment, quality of care giving or professional intervention contribute to the re-attachment process?

Smith and Howard et al (2000) identify two models they regard as dominant for understanding the process by which children with broken attachments may struggle to form subsequent relationships. The grief and mourning model (Fahlberg, 1994; Jewett, 1985) posits that lost attachments must be mourned successfully so that the unresolved feelings do not interfere with new relationships. The second model, the "negative working model" (Egeland, Sroufe and Erikson, 1983; Bretherton, 1987) holds that the internal representations children develop of their attachment figures and themselves become distorted if the carer is unresponsive, inaccessible or punitive. This perspective on the social world is carried forward into future relationships and may result in aggressive, controlling or avoidant behaviour towards the adoptive family. Developmental progress in the first will depend upon helping the child to re-visit the grief, bring feelings to the surface, and learn to manage the loss better. Progress in the second model will depend on how modifiable is the "mental blueprint".

In planning and establishing a new permanent family placement, it is crucial to assess what the child brings to the placement and how past experiences are likely to affect future relationships, especially the child's capacity to be parented. Hodges and Steele *et al* (2000) describe their work on narrative assessments, a technique developed at the Great Ormond Street Department of Psychological Medicine. They are interested in the way that the severely neglected or abused child is left with certain memories or "inner representations" of earlier family life. The method is designed to reveal the child's mental representations of self, others and relationships. The therapist aims to elicit, through play, representations of parent–child relationships. They are interested in representations of relationships as much as, or more than, memories of abusive incidents because it is these, they argue, that are likely to affect later relationships.

The therapist employs narrative stems for children aged between four and eight, which they describe as giving the child the beginnings of stories played out with doll and animal figures and inviting the child to show and tell what happens next. The child is not asked directly about his/her experiences as it is not intended to rouse the child's anxiety. Each story is rated for the presence or absence of about 30 themes or characteristics. It clearly takes much experience with both securely attached and maltreated children to complete the ratings and to reach sound conclusions on what they signify.

Although this approach has generated considerable interest, it is a fairly recent development and many questions remain. As these approaches rely very much on the acceptance of the concept of internal representations it is important to know whether they can be measured reliably and to what extent professionals can agree on the nature of these representations and on what they predict.

Psychodynamic and attachment theory models appear dominant in the US adoption literature, although a cognitive-behavioural model should also be considered a major contributor in the UK. In this model, difficulties with relationships are seen as learned patterns of behaviour which have been acquired in reaction to abnormal early experiences with caregivers. In treating disordered attachments, more emphasis is placed on modifying the undesirable or dysfunctional relationship behaviour. Roberts (2000), in describing her use of cognitive-behavioural therapy with adopted children, sees the task as identifying and removing the child's dysfunctional thinking patterns and teaching more adaptive strategies with the ultimate aim of achieving positive changes in the child's behaviour. This approach, it is claimed, is more likely to be appropriate and useful with older children with verbal skills.

Although not specifically concerned with adoption, Deblinger's (Deblinger and Steer *et al*, 1999) cognitive-behavioural work with sexually abused children is instructive. Their approach focuses less on helping children to vent sad or angry feelings and more on helping them to acquire skills in expressing feelings, reducing negative thoughts, correcting confused or inaccurate memories, and coping more appropriately with intense emotions.

An example of child psychotherapeutic work

The Tavistock Clinic has many years of experience in working with adoptive families and in their intervention model they involve therapists both for the parents and for the child who work closely together. The primary aim of the work is to support and facilitate the relationship between the parents and the adopted child/ren. Hopkins (2000) describes her child psychotherapeutic work as part of the overall service and provides a telling case example of the treatment of an adopted child with a disorganised attachment pattern. She describes how the child has no strategy for making contact with an adult when distressed and proposes that a punitive need to control the new parent underlies the child's opposition and defiance. She sees this disorganised behaviour as the result of the child's earlier failed attempts to seek attachment. In response, the child dissociates him/herself from the attempt to attach and this behaviour may become a fixed pattern. She describes how the therapist remains patient and tolerant in the face of the child's hostility and rejection and tries to interpret the hostile and distancing behaviour of the child. Therapy of this kind may need to continue twice a week for two years or more: clearly a rare and expensive commodity. This approach may be criticised on the grounds that the therapist's interactions with the child are used as a "trial ground" for the relationship with the new parent. This is very different from working directly to promote the growth of the relationship between the child and new parents and it is important to know which of these models of intervention is most effective.

For the reader who wants to turn to a much fuller account of attachment-based intervention, Hughes' book, *Facilitating Developmental Attachment* (1997), is a good illustration. Hughes raises the puzzling question as to why, when the abuse has been stopped, and the child has been removed and transferred to a new home, the child is not able to profit from the warmth and affection on offer but rather rejects and distrusts the advances of the new caregivers. Hughes takes the view that: 'Traditional interventions of play therapy, parent education and cognitive-behavioural techniques are not sufficient to effect sufficient progress with the poorly attached child'; they are neither intense enough nor compre-hensive enough. Hughes argues that it is necessary to go beyond tradi-tional child psychotherapy because trust of the therapist is hard to achieve and the child has limited capacity for engagement. He recommends new techniques to facilitate the child's ability to form new attachments. In work with the child he recognises the child's constant attempts to disen-gage and requires the therapist to keep finding new ways of maintaining engagement. He works therapeutically with the child but regards the promotion of parent–child attachment as the central goal and actively involves the parents in the therapy. He encourages the parents' affective attunement and empathy for the child's feeling state. He also sets out principles for parenting a weakly attached child.

Although apparently successful interventions with satisfied consumers are presented by therapists in their books, articles and at conference presentations, many questions remain unanswered. We do not know how many families rejected such a referral, or dropped out of therapy or were unhappy with the approach taken, and we have no independent evaluation of the outcomes compared with families not offered this intervention. It remains to be seen how cost-effective these interventions are with representative populations and how feasible it is to replicate them.

More radical approaches

Some therapists have put forward the view that traditional therapeutic approaches are not sufficient to have an impact on children who have been traumatised and who have disordered attachments. Howe and Fearnly (1999), for example, support the view that: 'Therapy with children with attachment disorder has to be close, intense, intrusive, nurturing and highly alert.' If children hold back positive feelings, avoid engagement and do not appear genuine in their expression of feelings, some believe more radical intervention is called for. One of these techniques is known as "holding therapy" (Welch, 1988; Cline, 1992; Keck and Kupecky, 1995; Levy, 2000). As practised at the Attachment Centre in Evergreen, Colorado, the child lies on the therapist's lap facing upwards and the therapist engages the child in eye contact. The therapist persists in holding the child when he or she struggles to escape. Anger is aroused in the child and holding is maintained but the child ultimately submits and this is followed by calm, caressing actions by the therapist. It is argued that the release of repressed emotion is essential to breech the defensive shield the child has erected and that this promotes attachment.

Many child psychotherapists and other adoption experts are implacably opposed to such interventions. James (1994) was one of the first to challenge holding therapy and some regard it as unethical and possibly re-abusive rather than therapeutic. Criticisms have been mounted both about the concept of Reactive Attachment Disorder and about unconventional therapies. Hanson and Spratt (2000) state that: 'Although a variety of treatments, some controversial, have been practised and disseminated at conferences and in the literature, none of these treatments have been subjected to rigorous scientific testing for either safety or effectiveness.' Barth and Miller (2000) argue that it is a grave error to be attracted to radical therapies that have no empirical support when there are conventional therapies that do have proven effectiveness and need only to be modified for use with adoption populations. Other therapists reject the holding technique itself but still argue that the child needs to revisit traumatic events in the context of a "nurturing, corrective experience".

It is essential to ask whether the children are genuinely suffering from a disorder that is related specifically to past *attachments* or to a variety of other adversities. For example, can lying and stealing be regarded as manifestations of disordered attachment or could there be alternative explanations? And if this is genuinely a disorder of attachment, does the theory lead logically to this confrontative and cathartic approach to therapy? One could argue that overcoming the child's resistance in this way does not contribute to a more positive view of relationships but to a feeling in the child of being over-powered by adults. This wish to break through the child's defensive stance may be a reflection of the parent's frustration at the child's unresponsiveness. Furthermore, is it likely that the absence of loving care can be replaced by anything other than the provision of consistent loving care? It is doubtful whether any brief intrusive intervention is likely to promote positive, enduring change.

There is a fair amount of evangelism in this field and it may be as well to take a more cautious and critical view at this stage. But if we do not have a safe, ethical, attachment-specific therapy which has proven cost effectiveness and which could potentially be widely available beyond the specialist centres, what can be offered? It may be best to give parents the best possible explanation of what is known about distortions in attachment, to examine whether the parenting style may need to be modified and to allow the repeated experiences of a stable, nurturing family life to create the environment in which a fresh attachment can develop. Specific social relationship difficulties can be identified (lack of eye contact, distancing, distortions in the display of affection) and the desirable behaviour reinforced by praise and attention.

Intervention with adoptive parents

The early literature on adoptive parenting focused on developing the necessary confidence and authority to parent an unrelated child. This remains important and practice papers talk of relieving the new parents' anxieties and uncertainties with encouragement to develop their own parenting style and to be less concerned to be perfect all the time. Katz

(1986) was one of the earliest to write about the difficulties of adoptive parenting, particularly being able to tolerate strong negative feelings, not giving up in the face of the child's rejection, and being able to find gratification in small incremental changes in the child's behaviour.

Practitioner accounts have exemplified a shift in attitude towards the adopters coming for help so that more of a partnership is created rather than expert direction. Kaniuk (1992), for example, puts the nature of the relationship between the adopters and the professional service providers at centre stage. She stresses the need to empower adopters and to treat them as capable, responsible adults and argues that the quality of relationship with the adoption worker is central to successful post-adoption support.

Despite the fact that it is likely to be the disturbed behaviour of the child which is most associated with placement instability, direct work with the child may not be the best approach. Ginsberg (1997), for example, advocates a shift from the focus on promoting changes in the child directly to a "parenting training" model of treatment where the parent is encouraged to act as therapist to the child. As we saw in the earlier section on the problems of the children, these can manifest themselves in a variety of ways. Parents may then have a need to develop better strategies for dealing with puzzling or challenging behaviour. Beyond information giving and general support, efforts may be made to modify parenting, not necessarily to make up for parenting deficits or distortions, but to develop different and more flexible responses. Coram Family is currently carrying out a series of Webster-Stratton-based parent training programmes (Webster-Stratton and Hancock, 1998) customised for groups of adoptive parents with research evaluation built in.

Parenting programmes have recently become more formalised. Adoption UK's parenting programme called *It's a piece of cake?* (Adoption UK, 2000) is a group-based and time-limited programme (eight sessions). The package, delivered by trained adopters, has a number of aims: support, information giving, facilitating new parenting strategies and anger management. The programme has yet to be independently evaluated, although it is always difficult to evaluate any multi-faceted intervention as it is hard to know which outcomes are related to which aspects of the intervention.

A paper by Hart and Thomas (2000) is concerned with the question of which aspect of the adoptive family system to address. They emphasise that attachment problems do not arise primarily from the adoptive family but from the child's prior experience. However, they regard the child's attachments as too new and insecure to justify direct work with the child. They do not think family therapy is appropriate as the families are not essentially dysfunctional and prefer indirect work with the new parents. Their aims are to reduce excessive professional–child contact, to strengthen the parent–child attachment and to create a secure base for adopters to explore what concerns them. They report therapeutic progress in work on a single case where improvement was shown, but it is not possible to say whether this was due to the intervention. Another approach with adoptive parents is put forward by Swaine and Gilson (1998). They describe a series of gestalt-based groups which encourage the parents to re-focus on their own needs and to create a safe, non-judgemental environment in which to express some of the pressures.

Although behaviour management programmes are now more widely available to birth families, reports of attempts to provide this service on a group or individual basis to adopters have only recently appeared in the literature. Although the paper by Pallett and Scott et al (2002) describes a project with foster carers, it is relevant to present it here. The team offers a ten-week group based training programme which aims to develop skills in managing difficult behaviour and to build positive relationships between the children and their carers. Using standard measures, they report on improvements in the emotions and behaviour of the children and a better quality of carer–child relationship. They acknowledge that a controlled trial would be necessary to demonstrate that it was the programme itself that made the difference.

Intervention with the whole family

Pinderhughes and Rosenberg (1990) have developed a programme called the Family Bonding Model, which is designed as an early preventive intervention involving the whole family. It lasts for 10 sessions and includes the children. A number of family group exercises are employed to draw out the family's feelings and expectations and to help everyone to understand the child's pre-placement history. After reviewing who should lead the family groups, they decided that an independent systems-oriented practitioner with no prior knowledge of the family should be engaged, as they thought there were too many complications with other workers already involved. Of the 50 families offered the programme, seven chose not to take it up, but this may have been because they felt they had adequate informal support. This intervention focuses on helping the child to attach to the parents, not to a therapist. Those who participated showed less need for services later on.

Gordon (1999) provides an example of a more structured programme specifically designed to help parents with children with disturbed attachments. Six group sessions one day per month were offered with the aim of exploring underlying reasons for their child's behaviour, especially anger. They explored the formation of attachment in adoptive families and looked for effective ways of intervening to help the child develop healthy attachments.

Bondy (1997) has conducted a rare experimental study of brief family psychotherapy with special needs children living with foster carers who wanted to adopt them; all the children were over seven. Forty-one families participating in the study received family therapy designed to assist the family to manage the transition of integrating the new child. The intervention was presented early in the placement while a control group of 20 received only limited caseworker support. The intervention was not randomly allocated but it was shown that the groups did not differ significantly on key variables. Comparisons at the follow-up, one year post treatment, showed that parent and child satisfaction was higher in the treatment group. Although fewer disruptions occurred in the experimental group, the difference was not significant. The author concluded that brief family therapy could not be recommended by itself as a means of supporting the placement. The study focused on measures of family satisfaction and did not address directly the level of the child's difficulties. It could be concluded that interventions that do not make reduction in the child's problem level the main target are unlikely to improve the quality of the placement and placement stability.

Table 1

Randomised controlled trials in intervention in foster care and adoption

Study	N	Participants	Intervention	Method	Outcome reported
Juffer and Hoksbergen et al, 1997 Stams and Juffer et al, 2001	90	Internationally adopted infants under five months placed with inexperienced families in Holland.	Use of behaviourally focused intervention with video techniques to enhance maternal sensitive responsiveness (between 5 and 12 months).	Random allocation to: No intervention control (n = 30) Personal book on Sensitive Parenting (n = 30) Book plus video Feedback Session (n = 30)	Significant main effect for book plus video on independent ratings of maternal sensitive responsiveness and secure mother–infant attachment. 7-year follow-up showed enduring effects in mixed families (with biological and adoptive children).
Myeroff and Mertlich et al, 1999	23	Adoptive families requesting help at the Attachment Centre at Evergreen. Children 5–14 years.	Multi-modal attachment based intervention including holding therapy.	Random allocation to: Treatment (n = 12) vs No intervention (n = 11)	Aggression and delinquency showed significant drop in CBCL[1] scores in treatment group. No change in controls.
Clark and Prange et al, 1994	132	Children (7–15) in foster care at risk for emotional and behavioural disorders.	Trained family specialist case managers recruited services mainly from existing social, health and educational provision.	Random allocation to: Experimental (n = 47) vs Routine Service (n = 62)	Significantly greater improvement found in behavioural and emotional adjustment over an 18-month period in the experimental group.
Minnis and Devine, 2001	182	182 foster children (5–16) and 121 foster families in Scotland.	Group programme aimed to enhance understanding and relationships between foster carers and children. Three days of didactic material followed by discussion.	Random allocation to: group-based training programme for foster carers designed to improve communication skills and attachment (57 families, 76 children) vs standard services (64 families, 106 children)	No difference immediately after training. At nine-month follow-up non-significant improvement in favour of the intervention group. When comparing self-esteem (MRS),[2] SDQ[3] and an attachment measure (RAD).[4] Intervention well received by foster carers.

[1] Child Behaviour Check List; [2]Modified Rosenberg Self-esteem Scale; [3]Strengths and Difficulties Questionnaire; [4]Reactive Attachment Disorder Scale.

Evidence of effectiveness

How far have the range of early and later therapeutic interventions in adoptive families shown that they can be cost effective? Do existing studies give good data on this question? It is an oddity that studies which ask whether levels of service are related to better outcomes often show that more services are related to worse outcomes (Rushton, 1999). That is simply because the most problematic and crisis-dominated cases attract services, but as the problems have usually become severe, the outcomes are usually poor regardless of the service. This will always be the case with cross-sectional studies and the need is for prospective studies to see whether one approach produces more favourable results over time, having started with equivalent groups. Very few examples of effectiveness studies exist in this field and even fewer use a robust design with cases randomly allocated to intervention and non-intervention groups.

The four studies listed in Table 1 are the only randomised controlled studies that could be traced, which bore any relationship to adoptive placements. They have been grouped together here because of their common experimental design, but with an acknowledgement that the studies are based on dissimilar groups of children and placements. Nevertheless, they have been summarised in order to show that such evaluative studies are feasible and, despite some inevitable shortcomings, are likely to produce more reliable and more instructive results than any other approach to evaluation.

Comments on evaluative studies

Two of these studies appear to have shown proof of effectiveness. In the Dutch infant adoption study, the use of video feedback to help mothers to observe and modify their behaviour towards their child appeared to be a strong factor in the success of the intervention. In the foster care intensive case management study, positive effects were demonstrated when families were helped to gain access to services. The Scottish foster care study did not show significant gains, perhaps because the group-based educational inputs were not sufficiently powerful to affect long-standing and severe difficulties in the children. Finally, the Evergreen study was small and had methodological weaknesses which prevented firm conclusions from being reached.

Further evaluative studies are urgently needed, although they need to meet at least the following criteria. They need to use a random allocation method taking care that it still meets ethical concerns; the interventions must have clearly defined targets; established pre-intervention and post-intervention measures that can reveal short-term change must be employed; the interventions must be well defined, replicable and without multiple components; sufficient numbers are required to perform comparisons of outcome measures and test for significant differences, and adequate length of follow up must be planned without involving too great a loss of cases to the research samples.

Summary

- The development of adoption support has been promoted through specialist centres, clinics and user-led organisations.
- The US has pioneered adoption preservation services but similar problems have been faced, such as uncertainty about secure funding, unevenness in the geographical spread of provision and little progress in discovering what works to sustain placements.
- Adoption services can be conceptualised as running from preventive to more problem-focused to therapeutic services.
- A wide range of interventions is being developed, including individual and group interventions with the placed/adopted children, with the adoptive parents and with the whole family. Which of these approaches is superior in which circumstances remains a largely unanswered question.
- Some advocate more radical interventions for problems that are considered unamenable to traditional approaches, although these have been criticised.
- Cost-effectiveness studies of interventions are rare and hard to conduct but future studies will need to meet strict research criteria in order to deliver reliable and useable findings.

4 UK Government policy and current initiatives

Recognition of the need

Obtaining post-placement and post-adoption services has in the past been left largely to the initiative of the parents to search for psychological, educational, health and other services, as far as services of an appropriate kind have existed. Recognition of the need for a comprehensive, accessible, adequately resourced, evenly distributed and effective post-adoption service has been slow to develop. Legislative backing for appropriate services in England and Wales dates back more than 25 years when the Children Act 1975 required local authorities to offer a comprehensive adoption service with counselling to be available for all parties. The Houghton Report (1972), which laid the ground for new adoption legislation, expressed concern about the lack of social work help in adoptive placements. In the subsequent Adoption Act 1976 (7 para 4.12) and the Adoption (Scotland) Act 1978, a duty was specified to provide post-adoption support. However, these rather general recommendations and requirements have been subject to wide interpretation and consequently have not led to adequate or equitable delivery of services.

Although the White Paper, *Adoption: The future*, issued by the Conservative Government in 1993 was welcomed, indeed thought to be long overdue, the most telling section stated that any improvements had to be achieved under the principle of "cost-neutrality". Adoption agencies were somewhat baffled as to how they could continue with their recruitment and placement services *and* develop an additional post-placement response without any augmentation of resources.

Hughes and Logan (1995) reported on two Social Services Inspectorate seminars which helped to draw attention to post-placement and post-adoption support. This was a pivotal development in publicising the concerns. The seminars were set up to examine obstacles to obtaining services, to explore the range and type needed, and to consider the implications for their delivery and management. It was becoming increasingly recognised that, with the more complex cases being encountered, more skilled professional advice and support was needed for adoptive parents. However, service innovations at this time were limited to small-scale projects and Hughes held that a lack of "strategic thrust" was responsible for slow development.

In 1997 the Social Services Inspectorate published *For Children's Sake* (Department of Health, 1997) which found, following an inspection of local authority adoption services, that much needed to be done in planning and reviewing their provisions and in placing adoption more in the mainstream of children's services.

The local authority circular, *Achieving the Right Balance*, issued in 1998 (Department of Health, 1998a), was the major lever to persuade SSDs, adoption agencies and voluntary organisations concerned with adoption, to review and improve their services. Only one paragraph, however, is devoted to post-adoption support, but in this it proposes that adopters should not be 'left with the feeling of being isolated'. It goes on to say that there should be a continuing 'partnership' between the agency and adoptive parents, particularly in the first few years following adoption. The extent to which new adoptive parents are able to detect this different type of proposed relationship and are aware of the benefits it should confer, needs to be researched.

In 1999, one of the Department of Health's *Messages from Research* books was published, collecting together findings from all the recent UK commissioned research on adoption (Parker, Ridgway and Davies, 1999). In the section on support, the satisfaction and dissatisfaction levels of the adopters were highlighted and also the problems in conceptualising 'demand for services' and 'satisfaction'. It was concluded that the need for support at different times and at different ages was still largely untouched by research.

Inspecting the quality of services

As a direct response to the circular *Achieving the Right Balance* (Department of Health, 1998a), the Social Services Inspectorate carried out a survey and inspection of English local councils' adoption services in 2000 and the findings were reported in *Adopting Changes* (Department of Health, 2000a). Data were gathered from 34 SSDs and inspections were conducted in 10 authorities. The report concluded that: 'There is little in place to assure the necessary support and assistance to adoptive families in the long term' (p 5). Commenting more specifically on post-placement support, the report lamented the lack of written information for adopters on the availability of specific services and the means of accessing them. It complained that many agencies lacked a detailed picture of who requested, and who received, services and led to uncertainty in the adopters as to what could be expected. The document stated that: 'following the adoption they [adopters] were left vulnerable to varying levels of service, and varying attitudes towards eligibility and priority'. The level of criticism aimed at local authorities was rising and the report concluded sternly that: 'This is clearly not an acceptable way to support the placement of some very damaged and vulnerable children' (p 61).

To the surprise of many in the adoption field, the Prime Minister, Tony Blair, then showed a personal interest and commissioned a Review of Adoption (PIU, 2000) and gave the responsibility to the Performance and Innovation Unit newly set up within the Cabinet Office. This was a radical shift in the level of interest shown by the Government in adoption. The Review followed on from the SSI enquiries in recommending that more clarity was needed about what a post-adoption service should entail: most notably that there should be greater consistency of service and more appropriate service locations. Recommendation 85 of the Review places a 'clear duty on the local authority to provide, or make arrangements to provide, comprehensive multi-disciplinary post-adoption services'. The term "duty" carries a serious expectation although it is still rather non-specific. For example, are requests for certain types of service to be privileged? Are all requests to be met regardless of seriousness? And is any sifting out permitted of problems that are not thought to be adoption-related?

Improving practice

The Adoption and Permanence Taskforce (England and Wales only) was also initiated at the time of the Prime Minister's Review, not, it was said, to constitute another form of inspection, but to help councils improve the performance of their adoption services. This is intended as a form of consultancy whereby a panel of professionals experienced in adoption in statutory and independent contexts bring their expertise and awareness of good practice to the local authorities. One aspect of its work is to review how local authorities are providing a comprehensive *post-adoption* service.

The Taskforce has developed an audit tool to assist in the assessment of adoption support by reference to a comprehensive list of possible services. Good practice materials have been made available for authorities seeking guidance on how to develop or improve services. It is uncertain how far these developments will lead to prescriptions being delivered to the authorities. For example, will there be direction as to which types of intervention are promoted or debarred, which services should be provided directly and which provided jointly or purchased from another provider, which services are regarded as cost effective and which families are entitled to a particular service? The work of the Taskforce could be highly significant in promoting an expansion of services and better communication and collaboration between relevant agencies. The most recent Taskforce report (Department of Health, 2001a) speaks positively of the way in which the local authorities that were initially targeted have been encouraged to draw up development plans, with the Taskforce helping to support their implementation. Having started with a small number of councils, the Taskforce is currently moving on to work with a larger number of authorities.

The experience of the Taskforce will be fed in to the implementation of the National Adoption Standards (Department of Health, 2001b), and practice materials will help authorities to achieve those standards. The draft practice guidance for National Adoption Standards for England (Department of Health, 2001c) states that: 'there will be access to a range of multi-agency support services before, during and after adoption. Support services will include practical help, professional advice, financial assistance where needed and information about local and national support groups and services'. A note of realism is welcome in the National Standards where it is acknowledged that placements may still be threatened by difficulties in the child and in interaction with parents' management styles *whatever the level of services*.

Furthermore, the Standards state that children should have independent access to services in their own right where they are of a sufficient age and level of understanding. In future, the child's concerns and difficulties should not be attended to only when an adult organises a referral. This is an extension of the principle of listening to children and it will be important to learn which services the children will choose and what they see as genuinely helpful, and to examine the part that choice has to play in the commitment to, and effectiveness of, whatever form of help is provided.

Although adoption does not figure very explicitly in the Government's Quality Protects initiative (England and Wales only) (Department of Health, 1998b) the first of the 11 objectives for children's social services is to ensure that children are securely attached to carers capable of providing safe and effective care for the duration of childhood. This clearly has implications for adoption services, and funds attached to Quality Protects can be used to serve this purpose (Rushton and Dance, 2002).

New legislation

Adoption is a devolved topic, so Scotland and Northern Ireland write their own legislation while England and Wales have common laws. Scottish adoption legislation has been updated more recently than in England by the Children (Scotland) Act 1995 which introduced a number of amendments to the Adoption (Scotland) Act 1978. In the Scottish Office guidance, published in 1997, attention is drawn to post-placement support including counselling and assistance to children who have been adopted, as well as for counselling for anyone else with problems about adoption. The National Care Standards for Adoption Agencies in Scotland (2002) promises to adopters a full range of support services after adoption and an Adoption Policy Review Group, convened in 2001, will be examining how law and practice can be changed to break down the barriers to adoption and to create an overarching framework for services.

In Northern Ireland, the Adoption (NI) Order 1987 and amending legislation contained in the Health and Personal Social Services (NI) Order 1994 requires social service boards and trusts to have responsibility for services to children who have been, or may be, adopted and also for birth parents and adoptive parents. A regional inspection has recently reviewed statutory adoption services, conducted a survey of adopters and made recommendations for improvement. The report is called *Adopting Best Care* (DHSSPS, 2001).

At the time of writing, a new Adoption and Children Bill is in committee stage in the English parliament and is likely to receive Royal Assent in 2002. This follows on from the Prime Minister's Review and will place a stronger requirement on agencies to provide support services. Concern was expressed that families had only a right to an *assessment* by social services and in the parliamentary debate the Minister argued that this clause was necessary, not in order to sidestep the intention to provide services, but to give the local authority the opportunity to assess need in relation to the responsibilities they were to carry for adoption support. The Government's intention to provide services and financial support was repeated. However, if the results of the promised assessment state that the needs do not cross an unspecified threshold, then the families will have to find their own services, as do any other parents seeking assistance from mainstream health, education and social care services. If the threshold is crossed but appropriate resources are still not forthcoming, then little has been achieved. Guidance being prepared for the new legislation and best practice advice will provide clarification.

In June 2002, the Department of Health issued a consultation document entitled *Providing Effective Adoption Support*. This was two years after the Prime Minister commissioned the review of adoption policy and practice. The Minister's introduction to the document states that 'adopted children and their new families should be able to access a planned package of adoption support services when they need them and for as long as they need them'. The consultation exercise will gather views on helpful forms of adoption support, on eligibility for financial support, and on improving access to services including education and health services. Once finalised, the framework of services proposed will be used to develop the regulations and guidance when the Adoption and Children Bill has received Royal Assent. We shall see, over the coming years, whether services of sufficient quality and effectiveness can indeed be developed, adequately funded, equitably delivered and properly co-ordinated.

Although many writers on adoption have lamented the slow progress and lack of a robust government response to calls for the development of post-placement support, few have theorised about the underlying reasons for this. Lowe (1997), however, proposes that there still exists a 'mind-set' whereby the birth mother offers her child to the adopters as a 'gift' and the adopters are then left to their own devices with no further state involvement. He argues that the old model, derived from baby adoptions where the legal adoption is a significant end point, is not appropriate for the very different modern practice of placing older children from care. He prefers modern policy and practice to be understood as a *contract* which carries obligations to provide *services* to set up the placement, and to provide support up to the adoption and beyond. It is evident that, the more this new model is accepted, the more progress can be made in specifying in greater detail what can and should be provided. Of course, accepting that these families are not "off the books" at all, but *entitled* to continuing services involving unknown cost, runs counter to the aim of reducing state child welfare costs.

Summary

- Progress in developing interest in adoption support services at local authority and central government level has been extremely slow in the UK until very recently.
- Scotland and Northern Ireland need more adoption support agencies. Messages from reports and inspections confirmed that post-adoption support was underdeveloped.
- Lack of certainty about a funding base has been a major obstacle.
- The appearance of the Prime Minister's Review, the Adoption and Permanence Task Force, Quality Protects funding, the new adoption legislation and the consultation paper on adoption services are all signs of a significant increase in interest and activity.
- New legislation will require, as never before, local authorities to make and participate in arrangements to provide adoption support services, including financial support.

Part 2
The UK Survey

5 Context and method

The context of the survey

The first section of this book has reviewed published material related to post-placement and post-adoption support. The history of the placement of children with special needs has been explored, looking at adopters' reports, practitioners' views of the kind of support needed, and agencies' experiences of trying to develop appropriate provision.

As has been made clear in the literature review, it has long been recognised that the factors most likely to threaten the stability of a placement are difficulties in the way that relationships develop between new family members and/or high levels of behavioural problems in the children. These problems are more likely to be present and more persistent when children are older at placement. Looked after children, particularly those who are older when placed for adoption, will always have experienced a substantial degree of loss and will often have experienced extensive periods of poor-quality parenting, for a variety of reasons. It is hardly surprising to find that their needs differ from those of children growing up with their birth families. Adoptive families too are dealing with their own challenges. Sometimes they will suddenly move from a status of child-free couple to parents of one or more children, complete with established personalities, in a matter of weeks. In other circumstances, they will be helping their birth children to adjust to new family members.

We have also seen, in recent years, a period of markedly increased interest from Government in the adoption of looked after children. This has been manifest in a number of initiatives and directives. These have been primarily targeted at English and in some cases Welsh authorities. Scotland and Northern Ireland have their own governance in this regard. However, personnel in these two countries would not be unaware of initiatives in England and Wales and elements of their experience will be similar. Certainly recent reports and guidance from both Scotland and Northern Ireland have emphasised the growing recognition of the need for adoption support (Scottish Office, 1997; DHSSPS, 2001; Scottish Executive, 2001).

As we have seen from the earlier literature review, although need has been recognised and the Government is encouraging change, there is not, as yet, any clear consensus as to what a comprehensive support service might consist of particularly where difficulties become severe. It is now a long time since Lowe and Murch *et al* (1999) conducted the fieldwork for their survey of support services and it seemed timely to investigate the current state of provision.

The aims of the survey

In this context the survey had the following major aims. First, to explore the ways in which local authorities and adoption agencies had responded to the challenge of improving adoption practice. Second, to catalogue the views of managers in the adoption field, across the UK, in relation to the level and type of support required for adoptive placements. Third, to explore current support services for adoptive families as provided by local authorities and adoption agencies. The final objective was to explore the availability, appropriateness and accessibility of services for adoptive placements that experience periods of difficulty.

As discussed in the literature review, support is a multi-faceted concept that many have struggled to define and quantify. In many circumstances, support is provided informally and often almost unnoticed by family members and friends. However, we are focusing here on services provided by public bodies and organisations that are designed to offer more formalised support specifically to adoptive families and their previously looked after children.

There are many strands to support. These include making sure that employers are supportive and that families have enough money and access to the information, help and advice that they need to deal with day-to-day living with the child. However, it is also true that many children, even among those who are older when placed, settle fairly quickly and fairly happily with their new families and need relatively little additional support. There is then a tightrope to be trodden between ensuring that appropriate services are available when needed, but that the autonomy and integrity of adoptive families are not undermined. It is important to learn how to facilitate without being intrusive.

Methods

The approach we used in this survey was to try to engage all social services departments (SSDs) and voluntary adoption agencies (VAAs) in order to obtain a broad overview of services across the UK. Each agency director (SSD or VAA) was asked to nominate the member of staff best placed to discuss provision of post-placement and post-adoption support in their area. These members of staff were then asked to participate in a 40-minute telephone interview at a time convenient to them. These interviews were semi-structured (see below), covered several aspects of placement support, and frequently led to the identification of dedicated or at least appropriate support services either within the agency or run by other agencies.

Sadly, although we had hoped to be able to do so, we were unable to include independent providers of adoption services and providers of appropriate services from other agencies in the sample. This was partly due to time pressure and partly because BAAF's publication of *The Adopter's Handbook* (Salter, 2002) pre-empted this endeavour. This being the case the information presented in the pages that follow, in relation to independent providers, is based on the comments and experiences of the adoption agency representatives who were interviewed by us. What appears should not be interpreted as either the official view of the agency concerned or as an independent assessment of the services provided.

When we set out on this journey, to map post-placement support in the UK, we had what, with hindsight, seems an over-simple understanding of how support might be organised and delivered. It rapidly became evident that we could not present people with a tick-list of services available in their areas and expect to learn much from it. The variety of provision and the variation in accessibility and quality would have rendered any such information largely redundant. What we have ended up with instead is largely a discussion document, which represents a snapshot in time of the development of adoption support services. Our respondents, all well-informed individuals in the forefront of service delivery, shared with us their hopes, their anxieties, their disappointments and their frustrations as they strove to improve services for adoptive families in their areas.

The sample

As stated, all voluntary and statutory agencies in the UK were approached. At no time did we expect all to participate, but we were delighted with the level of positive response that was received. The overall agreement rate among SSDs was 69 per cent. Figure 1 illustrates the variation in participation rates according to geographical region. This figure takes the regional definitions provided by the Department of Health (DH) for England. Wales, Scotland and Northern Ireland are each presented as single entities.

Figure 1
SSD participation by region

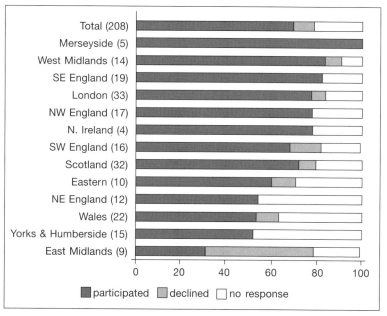

As is clear from the chart, very few authorities declined the invitation to take part, but several simply failed to return our reply slip. Some variation was apparent according to region as illustrated in Figure 1. By carving England into five major geographical sectors and including participation rates for Scotland, Wales and Northern Ireland, we found significant differences in response rates. Agencies in Wales and those based in the east and north-east of England were much less likely than other areas to agree to take part in the survey ($\chi^2 = 14.4$, df $= 6$, p<.05). The reasons are unknown since so few non-participating agencies responded at all. Of those that declined, the reasons given included little adoption activity, demand on staff time or the fact that they were undergoing restructuring.

For English authorities we had ready access, via the internet, to the national statistics on children looked after (Department of Health, 2002a). By this means we were able to compare participating and non-participating authorities on a number of key indicators. These included the numbers and rates of children looked after, the proportions looked after for more than two years and the proportions of children looked after who were placed for adoption or adopted from care each year. We found no significant differences on any of these indicators according to whether or not the authority agreed to participate in the survey. Neither were there differences in the ethnicity profile of looked after children as recorded on the Children in Need figures collected by the DH. Figures on some of these criteria were obtained for Wales via personal communication from the Statistics Office, from Scotland via statistics on the internet, and from Northern Ireland in paper report form (DHSSPS, 2001). Again no substantial differences were found. Of the nine local authorities that had recently been working with the Adoption and Permanence Task Force, six took part in the study. It was disappointing that one or two authorities that we know to be highly innovative did not take part in the survey. Although we do not have complete coverage of the UK, all regions are at least partially represented. We hope that by these means we have managed to trace all the substantial resources available to adoptive families and as far as we can tell there was no particular bias in terms of the levels of childcare and adoption activity in the agencies that responded positively.

Another way of looking at the data is to examine whether any bias existed in the types of local authority (LA) with regard to administrative arrangements. As shown in Figure 2, participation across administrative types was fairly similar. The lowest participation rates were among unitary authorities and in the "other" category. "Other" LA types, in this instance, include authorities in Scotland, Wales, Northern Ireland and the Channel Islands, for which these DH categories are not pre-defined.

Figure 2

The proportion of participating LAs by LA type

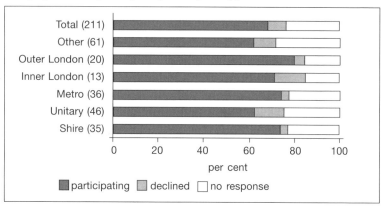

Figure 3

Distribution of local authority types

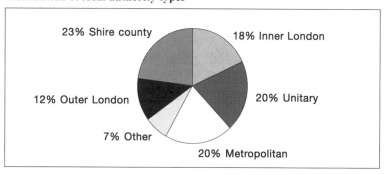

Figure 4

Distribution across regions

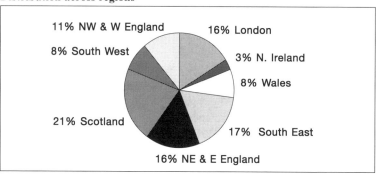

It will surprise no one to learn that, although permission was forthcoming from departments, it was not always possible to conduct the interview. Most of the people we talked to were very keen to discuss their experience and their ideas for developing practice, but some named individuals were repeatedly unavailable and it was not possible to identify another person to act in their place. In the end we spoke to representatives of 120 of the 133 local authorities that agreed to take part.[*]

Figures 3 and 4 show how the local authority sample was comprised according to administrative type and according to region.

The extent of participation by voluntary adoption agencies

Invitations were sent to 35 Voluntary Adoption Agencies (VAAs) throughout the U.K. These agencies were identified by means of BAAF's website. We have since discovered that one or two agencies are not represented on the website, it is unfortunate that this was discovered too late to contact them for interview. Where VAAs had several projects under one umbrella organisation (e.g. Barnado's and NCH), the headquarters only were approached initially. The Catholic Children's Society agencies, which each operate independently despite the frequent similarities in title, were approached individually. Twenty-three VAAs responded positively to the invitation to take part and all were interviewed. Two agencies declined and 10 failed to respond. These latter 12 tended to be smaller agencies.

Who did we talk to?

We did not collect data regarding age, sex or ethnicity of respondents, reasoning that this information was not especially relevant in the current context. We did feel that the type of post and level of seniority held by respondents, their length of experience and the degree of specificity of their job might influence the way in which they responded to our questions.

---

[*] A very small number of respondents participated by means of a self-completion questionnaire. In a couple of cases this was their preference; in others it was because the agreement of their authority was received too late to arrange an interview.

Within SSDs, for the most part, we spoke to team managers who were directly responsible for the day-to-day running of family placement or adoption teams (45 per cent). Quite often we spoke to service managers who had a somewhat broader overview (31 per cent), again usually on the placement-providing side rather than those more directly involved in children's fieldwork services. Sometimes we spoke to senior practitioners (17 per cent). Quite often these individuals would be taking the lead on adoption work within a generic family placement team. Just over one in five of our respondents were adoption specialists and a further 26 per cent worked with permanence through either adoption or long-term fostering. Around a third dealt with all aspects of family placement and the remaining 18 per cent had a broader remit across the whole of children's services. Very often this latter group were service managers, but several service managers had much more specific posts.

Among the voluntary agencies, we spoke to both directors or chief executives in the smaller agencies and team managers in the larger ones. The smaller agencies tended to be focused on adoption work, while the larger ones frequently had several other projects or units dealing with completely different aspects of community work.

A few respondents were relatively new to the management role or to the adoption field. However, most of those we spoke to had several years of experience in adoption work and many had been in their managerial posts for some time, although we grew very used to hearing about recent changes of job title! Overall, however, we were hearing from people with a wealth of experience in placing children with adoptive families, which informed their views and opinions.

Some differences of seniority were discernible between respondents. Those at service manager level tended to have a more grounded understanding of negotiations and planning at a more strategic level, but were sometimes less confident in answering questions related to practice on the front line. Those at team manager level often spoke more of personal contacts and experiences rather than "what the plan said". On occasion we spoke to a second person within an authority to clarify particular issues but on the whole all respondents were able to provide enough information for us to gain a broad understanding of practice in their area.

What did we ask about?

An interview schedule was designed specifically for the survey and questions were included on topics that seemed pertinent to our area of interest, either from our understanding of previous research findings, from the practice literature, or from a theoretical viewpoint. These were developed and refined with the welcome assistance of a representative of the adoption and permanence unit of the DH, an adoption specialist in a local authority setting and a chief executive of a voluntary adoption agency. As with the literature review, we had to be focused in our questions, and there are some areas, very pertinent to placement support as a whole, but not central to our topic, which we had to exclude. These were support services for birth families and adopted adults, intercountry adoption, step-parent adoption and the details of financial support. We focused specifically on services for adoptive families and their children, especially on services available when difficulties existed.

The first 20 SSD interviews were qualitative in nature and may be considered "pilot" interviews, although the contribution of these individuals has not been abandoned. However, we found very high levels of similarity of views on certain aspects and these questions were subsequently either dropped from the schedule or re-phrased to allow for pre-coded comparable answers. We shall make it evident where and how questions were developed subsequent to piloting as we proceed through the reporting of the results. The main thrust, however, was that early respondents felt that the organisation of services, procedures and practice developments in the early part of the adoption process along with the changing profile of children needing adoptive families were crucial to understanding support needs and service development in current adoption practice.

The eventual schedule therefore comprised questions that elicited the following information or views:

- the volume of adoption work within agency;
- current profile of agency's adoption work – changes in the profile of children needing adoption;
- organisation of adoption services within the department;
- post-placement and post-adoption services offered by the authority and how they were provided;

- links with other LAs, VAAs, consortia, health, CAMHS and education services, and other adoption organisations;
- services to support placements in difficulty.

Minor changes were made to the schedule to make it appropriate for use with voluntary adoption agencies.

Summary

- The aims of the survey were to:
  1. explore agency responses to the challenge of improving adoption practice;
  2. catalogue the level and type of support required for adoptive placements;
  3. explore current support services for adoptive families;
  4. explore the availability, appropriateness and accessibility of services for adoptive placements that experience periods of difficulty.
- The survey approached all LAs and VAAs in the UK. Almost 70 per cent agreed to take part. It was not possible to contact some nominated representatives and the survey is based on telephone interviews with representatives of 120 local authorities and 23 voluntary adoption agencies. Interviewees from local authorities were mostly service managers or team managers in family placement; those from VAAs were usually directors or chief executives of their agency.
- The interview covered a range of areas pertinent to supporting adoption but focused on services for adoptive families, particularly those experiencing problems.

6 Agencies' responses to the challenge of improving practice

The profile of adoption within councils and in senior management

To achieve effective change it is necessary that personnel throughout the organisation are engaged in the process. The enthusiasm of our respondents to the developments that were taking place in social services and social work departments was very evident for the most part, but we felt it important to establish whether they felt supported in this by senior management and council personnel.

Around 90 per cent of respondents felt that adoption practice had achieved a very high or a moderately high profile at senior management and at council level within their area.

There were about 10 per cent who felt that this was not the case. No particular pattern was evident as to which authorities fell into this latter category, although those in Northern Ireland, Scotland and Wales were less likely than those in England to feel that adoption was given *very* high priority.

Many respondents spoke about changes in either the structure or personnel in senior management, which had facilitated adoption work receiving a higher profile. Substantial changes had taken place in the organisation of service delivery teams (we shall examine these later), which were felt to be a result of increased interest but also allowed for further promotion of adoption activity at council level. A number of people spoke about their success in securing councillors' contribution to the adoption panels, and some mentioned regular liaison, including their giving presentations to councillors about their work.

In its report, *Adopting Changes* (Department of Health, 2000a), the DH had been critical of the level at which adoption and placement services were managed in many authorities. It was interesting to find, therefore, that of the service managers we spoke to, one-quarter of the posts were focused on adoption and/or permanence. The chain of command usually travelled only a short distance before reaching Assistant Director or Director level.

In 1998, Frank Dobson, the then Minister of Health, wrote directly to elected members of local councils reminding them of their responsibilities as corporate parents to children in local authority care. Some respondents mentioned this specifically and felt that to some extent at least the notion of corporate parenting was beginning to have an effect.

On what were our respondents basing their judgements? A good number felt that they had been less constrained in recent years with regard to inter-agency placements on financial grounds. The finance for increasing and refocusing teams had been found and other initiatives were beginning to materialise. Several authorities had set up forums that included senior staff from all relevant local authority and health departments as well as other involved or interested parties. These were designed to promote corporate parenting and were involved in strategic planning for "joined-up" services.

Overall, the majority of respondents did not give the impression of having been "bulldozed" into activities to which they were not inclined. Rather, people seemed to feel that the Government's initiative was long overdue and there was a sense of optimism and "can do" about the responses of most interviewees.

Funding issues

The corollary to all this enthusiasm and good news was predictably the question of resources and funding. Much of the development that had ensued had been achieved with special grants (for example, Quality Protects money in England and Wales) and under temporary initiatives. Even with these additions, most (65 per cent) felt that the size of the family placement team that was budgeted for was inadequate. For a small minority it was felt to be grossly so. One interviewee stated that she was leaving her post shortly because the job was 'undoable'. There was a tendency for authorities in England to feel this more acutely than other countries, although this was not statistically significant. There was no statistical relationship between the sufficiency of the team size and either the administrative authority type or the extent to which adoption was considered high profile. Thus, even those who thought they had the full backing of management and council felt under pressure.

Particular anxieties were expressed about the requirements of the anticipated legislation and guidance. In England, for example, in relation to the new Adoption and Children Bill, people were concerned about how the right to assessment for support might be interpreted and the implications that may have. There were also worries about how the placement targets and timescales for both assessment of adopters and placement of children might be achieved without skimping on the quality of preparation and support. The representative of one authority with an extremely good record on placements, and placements which were sustained, voiced this concern quite succinctly:

> There is this great emphasis on **quantity** and I'm worried about the actual problem, which is **quality**. I think the real performance indicator should be the disruption rate and I'm worried about the current push – especially in our area. This great thing on numbers, numbers, numbers. I'm not sure that that does the children good – at the end of the day they're not tins of baked beans. My fear with this current push in adoption is that we're going to have placements, placements, placements, disruptions, disruptions, disruptions and in about three to four years' time we'll decide adoption doesn't work and I think that's a shame and it's not correct. I do think the Department of Health ought to have included in their targets a disruption rate. It seems a pity that this isn't being taken into account.

Although Scotland and Northern Ireland may have had less in the way of government directives, there were similar pressures in these countries also.

The profile of the agencies' adoption work

In order to provide some context in which to ground the views and experiences of our respondents, we asked them to provide a little detail on the amount and type of adoption work they were doing. Our focus, of course, was on post-placement and post-adoption services for adoptive families and their children, and we wished, therefore, to gain access to data related to placement activity. We are aware that this excludes major elements, and perhaps the more important elements, of the overall role of family placement or adoption teams: those of recruitment, preparation and counselling for those who wish to search and work with birth families, for example. But, as always, time was limited.

We were anxious that the task of participating in the survey should not be too onerous for respondents. Therefore, in order to keep the effort of searching out statistics to a minimum, we asked for only one year's placement figures. However, within that we sought some detail on the ages of the children placed, whether they were placed with a sibling, their ethnic origin and whether any of them had significant disabilities.

Initially we sought to establish the proportions of children with learning difficulties or emotional and behavioural problems. However, because there is a lack of agreed definitions on these "diagnoses" generally, and authorities vary in the extent and/or manner in which they record such problems, this did not prove a useful area to explore. For example, some respondents told us how many children had educational statements while others tended toward a generalised assumption that all those of school age would be expected to have difficulty. Of course we could have asked our respondents to search through the files of each placed child to establish whether any statements or queries about development had been recorded but the exercise would have been tedious and probably not helpful.

It is perhaps enough to observe that this is a critical area with regard to support. A need clearly exists to move towards accepted understandings of different developmental and behavioural difficulties, better recording and thus a better chance of planning for appropriate provision of support services. It is something of a surprise that the "Looking After Children" materials, which allow identification of areas of difficulty, have not presented an opportunity to carry more information into aggregate record keeping systems.

The profile of children placed for adoption April 2000–March 2001

Of those authorities able to provide the figures we asked for, there was a wide range of placement activity in the year April 2000–March 2001. One authority placed no children at all and at the other end of the scale a large metropolitan area placed 81 children for adoption. Table 2 outlines the profile of placements made in relation to the age of children, their ethnic backgrounds, the proportion placed as part of a sibling group, the proportion who had a significant disability, and the proportion who were to be adopted by their existing foster carers.

On average, just short of one-quarter of placements were of infants under a year old. By far the largest proportion of placements was of pre-school children over one year but under five. Such children accounted for just under half of all placements made in that year. Anecdotally, a number of respondents mentioned that the larger proportion of this group would have been two- and three-year-olds. Of the remaining placements most (24 per cent) were of children between the ages of five and nine, while only 3 per cent of placements for adoption were of children aged 10 or over. The age profile for placed children was similar across authorities and regions. It was not possible to ascertain whether the very young children were usually being placed alone or as the youngest of a sibling group; anecdotal evidence suggests that both may be happening. Although some respondents reported somewhat more activity with regard to relinquished infants, this was not routinely recorded.

On average, 40 per cent of children entered their adoptive placement with a sibling. Some variation existed in the proportion of children placed with a sibling but not excessively so. Most authorities placed between 20 and 60 per cent of children with a sibling. Around 11 per cent of place-ments were of children from a minority ethnic background. Not surpri-singly, substantial differences were evident in the proportions of placed children from minority ethnic backgrounds. The proportions clearly reflected the local populations in the various areas with London, for example, placing a much higher proportion of black and dual heritage children than was true for most other areas.

Just 4 per cent of children placed for adoption were reported to have a significant disability: i.e. one that impaired daily activities. The diagnoses included cerebral palsy, moderate to severe Down's syndrome and some life-threatening illnesses. The incidence of disability among placed children was similar across regions. Just over 16 per cent of adoptive placements were in fact conversions from foster placements to adoption. This strategy has been promoted in various reports in an effort to reduce upheaval and secure permanence in children's lives, although, of course, it often means losing a foster family as a resource. Some variation in the extent to which this mechanism was used was apparent between authorities. For half of the authorities this process was used less than 10 per cent of the time, while for one authority it accounted for 75 per cent of the placements made in that year. These differences, however, were not significant.

Table 2

The profile of children placed for adoption April 2000–March 2001

Criteria	Mean	Range	Standard Dev.	From Ivaldi 2000
Number placed	19.77	0–81	15.3	
Proportion under 12 months	24.6%	0–73%	15.0	25%
Proportion 1–4 years	49.1%	18–100%	18.1	54%
Proportion 5–9 years	23.2%	0–63%	14.1	}21%
Proportion over 10 years	3.5%	0–40%	7.4	}
Proportion placed with a sibling	39.4%	0–85%	20.4	37%
Proportion from minority ethnic background	10.5%	0–60%	13.8	10%
Proportion with significant disability	4.2%	0–40%	7.3	N/A
Proportion foster placement conversions	16.5%	0–80%	18.7	13%

These figures are remarkably similar to those reported by Ivaldi with reference to adoption orders granted in 1998/9 (Ivaldi, 2000). The age profile in the current survey was a little older with a slightly higher proportion of placements of children from a minority background, with slightly more placed as part of a sibling group and with a slightly higher proportion of foster placement conversions. At first glance, the fact that the age profile was older in this survey than that reported by Ivaldi seems to run counter to respondents' perceptions of children being placed earlier in recent yeart. But the difference is not large and it may well be accounted for by the fact that although the data from Ivaldi presented above concern characteristics at placement, the sample was based on completed adoptions. It seems plausible that this discrepancy can be explained by the possibility that some of the placements of older children made prior to 1998 did not proceed to adoption order and were, therefore, not represented in Ivaldi's sample.

Changes in the profile of children placed for adoption

We asked about changes in patterns of placement in recent years. We were particularly interested in change since the issuing of the DH circular LAC, 98/20 which went to all English authorities in August 1998 (Department of Health, 1998a).

Over 56 per cent of authorities reported a very marked increase in the number of children being placed, with a further 22 per cent noting a gradual increase over time. Of the 22 per cent who did not detect an increase, many were Scottish and Irish authorities where the emphasis on adoption has been somewhat less than is the case in England and Wales. Other authorities reported that adoption had long had a high profile within their departments and pre-existing high rates of placement were simply being maintained.

Authorities most likely to see a marked increase were unitary authorities and metropolitan areas. While it is possible that some authorities of this type had previously been under-performing in relation to planning for looked after children, it is also plausible that other explanations are pertinent.

Where appropriate, we asked respondents to outline their perceptions of why they had seen an increase in adoption activity. A number of important features emerged from this question. We shall visit them briefly here but many are worthy of more discussion and will be dealt with in more detail in later sections. The responses fell into four broad categories.

First, and perhaps fundamental to most of the others, was a perception of a change in the "culture" of social work with adoption being more broadly recognised, throughout the organisation, as a positive option for children. This is not to suggest that it was the only option. It was widely recognised that there were other alternatives that might offer a more appropriate permanence for many children.

Many felt that the pendulum swing towards keeping birth families together, which followed the implementation of the Children Act 1989, was on the return. They felt there was more structured and more rigorous assessment of birth families, with time limits on rehabilitation, much tighter planning for children already accommodated, and earlier examination of permanence options. Parallel planning for children was in evidence (a process in which permanence options are explored while assessment and proceedings continue) and some spoke of moves toward concurrent planning. This is a model by which children are placed with prospective adoptive families while assessment and care proceedings run their course on the understanding that they will either adopt or accept the child's return home – depending on the outcome of proceedings (Katz, 1999). Overall, the survey revealed a substantial tightening-up on the process of looking after children.

The other factor that was frequently mentioned to explain the increase was structural and organisational change, designed to facilitate the new modes of practice. Comments like 'the increase followed the establishment of the permanence teams', or 'the dedicated adoption team' were frequent. These activities were often felt to be complemented by changes in the structure and focus of family placement teams and indeed by raised public awareness that led to more fruitful recruitment campaigns.

Together, these three factors were reflected in more children coming through the system via care proceedings, and in children being dealt with more quickly once in the system. Some authorities felt they had also been dealing with some children who had been stuck in the system previously.

There were some additional considerations which respondents felt were contributing to the increase: e.g. factors that might be particular to certain areas. These were an increase in the number of drug-using parents and mental illness among parents, either of which often resulted in young infants or children requiring placement.

While the speedier planning for children was welcomed by many of the respondents, some corollary comments are worth noting. Concern was expressed about the prospects for children who were "waiting" but were already "older". Many managers talked of the continuing difficulty to find families for older children, for large sibling groups and particularly for boys of seven or eight. These difficulties were felt to be compounded by the "availability" of younger children. In the words of one respondent:

> For years we had largely counselled people out of the pre-school age group. But if you want a child and there is a choice between a child of two and one of seven, most people will choose the two-year-old – people want as much of a child's childhood as possible.

This throws up the question of what is happening currently to those older children who are waiting. We can only speculate. With hindsight it would have been helpful to ask about the profile of children waiting as well as those being placed, but this falls outside of the strict aims of the study.

It was also noted that many respondents commented on the continuing difficulty of finding appropriate families for children with a minority ethnic background, particularly children of mixed heritage. Another question that arose on occasion was whether the Government's adoption agenda was always the right option for children. One or two respondents expressed concern and dismay at 'the sheer number of children growing up away from their own families'.

A final note on these points concerned the activities of the courts and legal proceedings which were still experienced as a source of serious delay at all stages of the process. This issue has received attention before, and although Government has acknowledged the need to move forward on the legal process, nothing has yet emerged to make a difference. However, one respondent spoke about a change in personnel in the legal system in their area, which had made a significant difference to the speed with which applications were being processed. Prior to this change, cases had taken years; then suddenly adoption orders were beginning to come through in months. Although this is only a single example, it perhaps serves to highlight the point that the attitudes of individuals in senior positions can be critical to the success of innovation. We saw earlier that similar comments were made about councillors and senior managers, and the theme returns later.

Summary

- The majority of LAs reported that adoption had achieved a high profile within their authority. This was more true in England and Wales than in Scotland and Northern Ireland.
- Concern was voiced about staffing levels and resources, particularly in light of the impending legislative changes regarding adoption support and the need to achieve placement and applicant assessment targets.

- LAs varied widely in both the number and proportion of looked after children placed for adoption, but most detected an increase in the rate of placement for adoption at least since 1998/9.
- Many thought the age profile of children requiring adoptive placement was changing and children were younger. This was perceived to be due to tightening up on decision making and planning and because better mechanisms were often in place to speed up the process of panel hearings and referral for family finding.
- Important considerations arising from the discussion of placement patterns and profiles included:
  - continuing difficulty in locating families for children of minority ethnic background, for older children and particularly for boys;
  - an increase in the proportion of children requiring placement because of parental substance misuse or mental health problems and the uncertainty about potential effects on the children's subsequent development, and therefore future needs;
  - whether adoption was always the right choice for individual children;
  - what was happening to older children who were already waiting – since younger children had been available;
  - the continuing delays resulting from court proceedings.

The level and type of need among adoptive families

As noted previously, many respondents had observed an increase in the rate of placement. In England and Wales this was felt to be largely due to raised awareness, re-organisation of children's services and tightening up on planning and decision making. Some felt that older children were being placed, although most indicated that the children they were family finding for tended to be younger. A number commented that more sibling groups were needing families. Even though an increasing number of younger children were being placed, respondents felt that many of them were still likely to require services. These younger children were often from back-grounds and families where there had been substance misuse, mental health problems or abusive or neglectful parenting. Uncertainty was expressed as to how these children may develop and thus what their support needs may be in future.

Anxieties were felt about the pressure to increase numbers and to speed up processes and the possibility of this resulting in inadequate preparation of both children and adopters or poorly judged decisions. Such an outcome may of course lead to an increase in the rate of disruption.

In early interviews we tried to obtain estimates of the proportion of children requiring placement who had behavioural, emotional or relationship difficulties and also the proportion of families that representatives expected would need services beyond the routine. However, we found it very difficult to elicit such information. Clearly there is a need for managers to be able to quantify the extent of difficulties in a standardised way in order to plan for appropriate provision.

Respondents varied in their views about the services they felt to be most critical. It is likely that these reflect the types of children that they are placing although there was no evidence of this from the information available to the survey. It is also possible that their views relate to the level of provision of post-adoption support made by either their own teams or on their behalf by means of service level agreements with other service providers.

The areas of greatest need in the post-order period, according to respondents, were help with contact arrangements with birth family members, help with searching, and help for behavioural or relationship difficulties from psychological services. But perhaps the most telling point concerning post-order work was that respondents did not know what the demand was likely to be. They did not want to raise people's expectations and then not be able to deliver. Some of the more advanced authorities were in the process of researching their own adopters to learn what kind of support they required. The respondents, it appeared, felt they were only seeing the tip of the iceberg.

The organisation of local authority children's and family placement services

The organisation of services and the mechanisms for service delivery have received little attention in the literature review, which concentrated on service content rather than delivery. We include it here because pilot interviews suggested that aspects of organisation were critical to service provision and it forms a major part of local authorities' responses to the need to improve services (our first stated aim in conducting the survey). The Social Services Inspectorate (SSI) for England and Wales has written extensively, and often critically, of the way local authorities divide and deal with their responsibilities. Over time the received wisdom tends to swing backward and forward, between specialist or generic, task-focused or area-focused practice. The thrust of SSI reports in recent years has been towards a greater degree of specialisation with oversight and planning for children's services being dealt with at a fairly senior, but not remote, level of management (Department of Health, 2000a).

We were struck immediately when we began the survey by the frequency with which agencies were restructuring and reorganising. At some points it seemed that almost every authority we spoke to had been, was being, or was about to be reorganised. Sixty-eight per cent had experienced reorganisation within the preceding year, mostly in England and Wales.

However, local authorities have mainly continued to have teams of social workers statutorily responsible for the children, and resources teams, which provide placements when needed. But within that broad division, substantial change was taking place. This was often true of both children's and family placement services. The variety of arrangements was remarkable, but generally the thrust was toward a greater degree of specialisation, on both the children's and the family placement side.

Children's services

Only around 20 per cent of local authorities we spoke to continued with generic children's and families teams. Around 40 per cent had moved to teams that dealt with looked after children and 15 per cent had teams specifically concentrating on children requiring permanence. The remaining 25 per cent of authorities divided their resources up somewhat differently: some preferring to focus on children according to their age, others according to whether their need for services was likely to be short- or long-term.

Clear differences existed between authorities in terms of their scope for specialisation, according to their size and the populations they served. A metropolitan team, with a sufficient staff quota and a high population density, will find it easier to divide along task-focused lines than will a small authority that has few staff to start with or authorities that cover large rural areas with very low population density.

The obvious advantage, according to our respondents, in moving towards a focus on children who need permanence is the potential for skills and knowledge to develop in that particular area. Several respondents were quick to point out that, within the local authority, permanence was not synonymous with adoption and that it could also be achieved through a residence order, foster care and kinship care. Nevertheless, there will be some common needs among children separated long term from birth parents and the skills needed by workers who deal with such children might be only rarely used in a generic post.

The emergence of teams for looked after children may represent a slight dilution in terms of specialisation, in contrast to the permanence teams, but this still offers an opportunity to focus on skills needed to work with separated children and to develop expertise in assessment and planning for them.

The drawbacks included the narrowing of experience opportunities for social workers. But CSWs, whose remit is generic, continue to try to deal with the pressures of child protection work, emergency and duty work, court appearances, locating accommodation, and a host of other tasks. It is not surprising that these factors detract from workers' ability to push forward on planning and acting for children who are (or should be) "already safe in foster care".

It is increasingly recognised that preparation is potentially one of the critical features of a successful adoptive placement. This is true for preparation of both parents and children. This topic, although very important, is not central to our focus in this survey but it does touch on organisational aspects. Much has been written about whether generic CSWs are able to ring-fence the time necessary to either do the work or indeed to develop the skills needed to prepare children effectively. For some time there have been calls for moves towards specialisation in this regard. We were interested therefore to learn that, in the great majority of cases, the preparation of children remained the responsibility of the CSW, regardless of the type of childcare team which operated. There were a few exceptions to this and in these cases respondents felt that their alternatives conferred significant benefits. We outline these arrangements later when we examine joint working between children's and families' social workers.

Family placement services

Family placement services too were being reorganised. Over 85 per cent of family placement teams were centralised within the authority. Those that retained area-based family placement services were almost exclusively shire counties. Scotland and Northern Ireland were also likely to have centralised teams.

The majority of authorities had also introduced a degree of specialisation into the family placement services. It was rare indeed to find teams who dealt with all placements including residential (just 9 per cent). Around one in five of respondents reported a dedicated adoption team and a similar number worked in dedicated permanence teams, including adoption and permanent fostering. Just over one-third of teams continued to work with all aspects of family placement and in around 15 per cent of SSDs there were adoption or permanence specialists within a generic family placement team. In some teams (of all types) there was specialisation according to task. For example, some authorities chose to have staff specialising in recruitment and advertising, or focusing on assessment or support. Other authorities preferred an approach that allowed each worker to perform a little of all tasks.

A word of caution, however, was proposed by one manager who headed a small team which had been specialised into either adoption or fostering. A combination of circumstances had led to a time in which all of the adoption posts were vacant. This had left a vacuum which workers on the fostering side were hard pressed to fill, not only in terms of time but also knowledge and experience. This manager was rapidly moving back towards a generic family placement team to avoid a reoccurrence.

Post-adoption teams

One of the tasks that has come to the fore throughout the UK is that of post-adoption support (although the emphasis may change following the most recent consultation document issued to English authorities by the Department of Health (2002b). Many local authorities were seriously concerned about post-adoption services and a number had put in place post-adoption teams. Around 10 per cent of the respondents stated that their post-adoption team had been in place for some time. A further 25 per cent reported that this had been put in place within the last year and 10 per cent were anticipating such a development imminently. Of the remainder, a minority were hoping for approval or funding to implement such a project but most had no such plans. In England and Wales, those who had no intention of introducing post-adoption specialists fell into two camps: either it was a proposal that had been discussed and decided against on the basis that specialist experience and expertise may be lost, or the decision had been taken to out-source this aspect of the service. In Scotland and Northern Ireland, specialist post-adoption workers or teams were rare and no contracting-out of post-adoption services was recorded.

Of those who had dedicated post-adoption teams, half had at most the equivalent of one full-time worker. For the most part, the tasks that fell to post-adoption workers divided into three major types. The first concerned the management of letterbox arrangements or birth record counselling and searching. This was particularly true for some of the more established posts. The second concerned the development of ongoing training for adopters, the formation of support groups, and gathering and disseminating information both for authority use and to develop information leaflets for interested parties. The third aspect was a desire for post-adoption workers research local needs and then to advise on the development of services. On relatively few occasions did the respondents spontaneously discuss the role of the post-adoption worker in relation to casework with adoptive families. We shall return to post-adoption work when we examine the provision of support services later in the text. Before doing so we will complete our review of organisational factors by exploring views on joint working between children's and families' workers.

Joint working between children's and families' social workers

This was one of the topics we touched on in the early interviews and it was frequently referred to in later interviews too. It must be remembered that we were usually talking to managers or practitioners from family placement, rather than the children and families teams, and so a rather biased viewpoint may emerge. Nevertheless, it seems valuable to convey their impressions. Throughout the UK, in almost all agencies, both types of worker tend to be involved in the majority of adoptive placements and one CSW and one FSW will often work together quite intensively to facilitate a child's placement with, and eventual adoption by, a new family. The way in which this joint working is negotiated and implemented can be significant for the placement.

In the past, CSWs have been perceived as having too little time to devote to children in permanent placement, having divided loyalties between the interests of the child and those of the birth family, and of having little opportunity to acquire the necessary skills and knowledge to progress adoption plans efficiently. With the change in attitudes reported earlier, these factors may now be less evident.

Where problems were detected, the majority of respondents spoke of understaffing, rapid turnover and pressure of work for CSWs.

[I think the fact] that the number of children in the LAC popula-tion is high has an impact on the ability of childcare workers to fulfil their role. Pressure leads to frustration for those working in family placement. Making sure that the child is prepared is at the root of any difficulties between teams. Often FSWs will take on the responsibilities.

There are major problems in our current crisis situation. Not every child has a social worker. There is a willingness to work together but the other demands take precedence. It is often left to FSWs to push plans along. Once placed [with adopters] they are perceived to be safe.

A related but slightly different matter concerned inexperience and lack of knowledge in adoption work in CSW teams. This could still mean that CSWs did not make or pursue plans as quickly as possible especially where team managers on the fieldwork side were less knowledgeable about the adoption process.

Some respondents felt that tensions could occur between service groups with professional competitiveness and disputes occurring about who was driving the care plan.

The issues regarding joint working are down to communication pro-blems. Family placement workers are not routinely invited to reviews. We need systems for joint working.

*I think there are sometimes problems with different perspectives, part-
icularly where social workers haven't had an awful lot of experience
around adoption and sometimes it feels that they need some additional
help and advice and information. I think that sometimes they kind of
go off on a bit of a tangent, because they don't really understand what
the issues are around permanence for children through adoption.
An example of that would be contact plans where sometimes a direct
contact plan is considered for a child who is very, very young –
e.g. under 18 months, where that doesn't really fit with some of the
permanence concerns for the child.*

So, occasionally, it seems, there remain problems about lack of time, lack
of experience or knowledge, and lack of communication and clarity. In
many authorities these concerns were being addressed as far as was
practical. We have already seen that a large number of authorities were
moving toward increased specialisation in children's teams. Respondents
felt this would provide those CSWs with the opportunity to develop
understanding and skills in relation to adoption or permanence work.
Other moves were also taking place in training programmes and in setting
up procedures and systems to ensure liaison between children's teams
and family placement teams which would provide an opportunity to seek
advice as necessary.

Training in adoption work for children's social workers

Almost everyone we spoke to bemoaned the lack of training for
CSWs in adoption work. It was not seen as a core training need in most
training departments and many other topics were in competition for
a slice of the training budget. The responses of two-thirds of our interviewees suggested that this area needed development in their agencies.
However, 15 per cent of agencies described what seemed to us to be
very good practice. For the most part these respondents, or members of
their teams, had taken it on themselves to develop training packages
that would assist CSWs in their role in relation to adoption. Although
most were relatively new developments, it was usually envisaged that
these packages would either be a rolling programme, or be integrated
with the induction procedure for new staff. They mostly concentrated

on the process of adoption and on dealing with courts, but would still provide vital information.

An element of dismay was noted from some respondents who had found the take-up of optional training among CSWs to be poor, although it is to be anticipated that, as specialisation takes hold, and for some workers adoption becomes a core task, this will become less of a problem.

Some of the larger consortia also provided appropriate training for children's workers. One interviewee was in the process of conducting an Adoption Skills Audit in which social workers felt they needed more training in courtroom skills, more help on preparing children for adoption and more general training on the adoption process.

Systems and procedures to improve communication

Respondents told us that it had been the case that they would not hear about children needing placement until plans had moved quite a long way down the line. Very often the children may already have been looked after for some time before this point was reached. This caused a tension between adoption agency procedures and the courts because the Adoption Panel was being asked to approve plans that had already been decided in court. Following the various initiatives, particularly in England and Wales, systems had very often been put in place to ensure that family placement or adoption teams were aware of children needing placement.

Several individuals spoke about formalised procedures for notification of family placement units. These would sometimes come through as early as the first review.

In a number of cases workers from the family placement team were routinely invited to reviews, in others they would be invited to reviews where permanence was likely to be discussed, in still others they would attend all six-month reviews where decisions needed to be made. Most of the agencies commented that they allocated an FSW to each child with a permanence plan as soon as the decision was made, which allowed both an overview of progress and a more detailed knowledge of the child for whom they would be trying to find a new family.

One respondent mentioned an initiative designed to make permanence a joint responsibility from the moment the decision is reached.

Eighteen months ago we set up a consultation forum. This is a monthly event. It is chaired by the team manager, and attended by the child psychologist and post-adoption worker. The expectation is that CSWs will bring cases to this forum as soon as the decision for permanency has been made. We want to help them to think about contact issues, the child's needs post placement and any likely difficulties. It is heavily over-booked every month now. It was slow to start with but the feedback has been very positive indeed.

We asked about liaison opportunities between CSWs and family placement teams for those occasions when advice may be needed *before* decisions about permanence had been reached. Almost all of the managers felt that there was sufficient opportunity for this, although some detected some resistance and felt it was not always used. However, there was substantial variation here. A number of respondents felt there was sufficient opportunity because staff shared the same building, or even sometimes the same office. Others described mechanisms that had been specifically developed to encourage liaison and thus facilitate more appropriate planning and the achievement of necessary tasks in the permanence process.

Some authorities had developed a practice of allocating an adoption or family placement specialist to each of the appropriate children's teams so that CSWs had an immediate and known contact person in family placement. Others had developed practices like "surgeries" for children's social workers, whereby a member of the family placement team (usually a senior member) would be available in the children's teams on a regular basis for consultation. These moves were felt to be beneficial both in offering children's workers access to the team's knowledge and expertise and in allowing the family placement workers very early awareness of the children for whom they may need to find placements.

A few authorities had abandoned joint working altogether. As soon as a decision for permanence was made, the statutory responsibility for the child transferred to a worker in the family placement or adoption team.

We have an unusual set up in that as soon as proceedings are ended, one of our workers takes over the statutory responsibility for the child and progresses the placement from the CSW viewpoint. There may be occasional problems in that if we are short of staff it can end up being the same worker for child and family. This can work OK if there are no problems but can cause tensions if the placement runs into difficulties. Our reason for doing this is that it became evident that CSWs were unable to prioritise adoption work. We found that the descriptions of children on Form Es were often very inaccurate and out-of-date and the team felt that their family finding could be much more successful and much more targeted if they knew the child for whom they were family finding.

[Question: Is it working?]

Our disruption rate is reasonably low, so probably yes. Also we find that when we work with other LAs we find a wide variation in the level of expertise and knowledge regarding adoption work. Where the traditional pattern exists, with the family placement social worker only "finding" the adoptive family, we find interagency placements hard work once the placement is approved by Panel. On the whole there is less input from the child's social worker. We have had to make strident representations on occasion to achieve a satisfactory level of input regarding statutory visits, reviews, life story work and so forth because of other child protection pressures and a perception that, once placed for adoption, the job is virtually complete.

This individual, and others who described similar models of working, all felt that this practice provided great benefits for the children, their adoptive families and often for birth families too. There are of course similarities between such a model and the increased specialisation in children's teams which we described earlier, whereby some agencies are moving, or have moved, to permanence teams in children's services. The drawbacks are a necessary change of social worker for the child, meaning another disrupted relationship. However, given the frequency with which we heard about the high turnover in children's teams, it seems likely that many children would face changes in social worker whatever the model, and the increased time for adoption and understanding of it can only be good in the long run.

Voluntary adoption agencies

Thus far, we have concentrated on local authority structures and organisational developments. Much of what has been covered is less relevant to voluntary adoption agencies because of the different ways in which they work. The majority of VAAs concentrated entirely on adoption and most were organised in only one team. About half had chosen to establish specialist post-adoption teams and half had not. The reasons for not doing so were similar to those voiced by LA managers. Almost all of the agencies recruited a pool of adopters, very few accepted referrals of children who needed a family to be found as a matter of routine. Although some were prepared to undertake preparation work with children, most expected this work to have been done prior to linking with a new family. The teams themselves were considered extremely experienced and dedicated to their task. VAAs reported less difficulty with staff recruitment.

Summary

- Substantial reorganisation has taken place within most social services departments in England and Wales, although this is not the case in Scotland or Northern Ireland.
- Reorganisation often involved both children's fieldwork teams and family placement services. In both cases the trend was towards increased specialisation with the formation of looked after teams or permanence teams on the fieldwork side and permanence or adoption teams on the family placement side.
- Specialisation was usually perceived to be beneficial in terms of a better service to children and their adoptive families and in terms of encouraging expertise in staff but with an acknowledgement that this necessarily reduced the range of experience opportunities for staff.
- Around 40 per cent of authorities had or were anticipating the creation of post-adoption teams. Of the other 60 per cent, around half had decided against this degree of specialisation, thinking that post-adoption work provided an important learning opportunity which fed into work with families who were just beginning the process. The other half had elected to contract this element of the work to an independent organisation specifically set up to provide services. The advantages

claimed was that the service was comprehensive, specialist, independent of social services and offered by staff who had the chance to develop expertise.

- Communication and liaison between CSWs and FSWs workers were identified as key issues in both making and supporting placements. Mechanisms had often been put into place to encourage improvements

- Much more training was needed for children's workers. There was optimism that such training would be more relevant to social workers specialising in working with looked after children or in permanence and that opportunities might therefore be better exploited.

- Recruitment and retention of staff are known to be longstanding and significant problems in children's teams, but respondents identified increasing difficulty in recruiting to family placement posts also.

7 Current support services:
Routine and specialist

Who should provide support?

An increasing expectation exists that all adoption agencies will provide a comprehensive post-adoption service; in the words of the most recent Department of Health consultation document, a '*comprehensive adoption support service*' (Department of Health, 2002b). This document recognises that modern adoption is a lifelong process and that the granting of the order does not necessarily mean any change or lessening in the amount or type of support that is needed.

What stage of development, therefore, have local authorities reached? One respondent summed up their starting point three years ago in this way:

> *Up until the adoption agenda hit, the only support we really provided (after order) was allowances to those who qualified. I am sure it was the same everywhere. People disappeared unless and until they had to come back because of breakdown.*

She went on to describe what had been achieved in the interim and the hopes and ambitions of their department for the future.

Indeed, this survey confirmed that a good deal of progress is being made in local authorities across the UK. Developments are a moving target, which made it difficult to categorise and group activities. What may have been true for any particular authority on the day of interview may well be subject to change the following week or month, as departments restructured or new agreements came into force with other agencies.

Although looked after children are the responsibility of specific social services departments, and may be placed with families recruited by the same department, they can also be placed with families recruited by a variety of different adoption agencies, both local authority and voluntary. The policies of the specific agency involved and the service agreements between the child's agency and the family's agency will determine much of the way in which support is offered. Thus, both the child's agency and the family's agency are likely to be involved in offering direct support until the adoption order is made. In addition to this, services may be offered by the placing authority and/or outsourced to a variety of public and voluntary bodies. Agencies vary in the degree of expertise available within their teams and no consensus exists, as yet, on the level of skill or knowledge that should be the minimum for an adoption worker.

Service level agreements and purchasing arrangements

The means by which local authorities arrange for provision of services can vary. It is possible for them to make "spot purchases". Thus if a family needs a particular type of assistance, perhaps some one-to-one counselling, or attendance at a special training group, this may be arranged and paid for on a one-off basis. Alternatively, an authority may decide that the needs of a particular group of service users or type of service in its entirety may be better provided by another agency. In this latter case, the authority may make a service level agreement with the agency, indicating that they will undertake to pay for a set level of service throughout the course of a year. This arrangement means that the voluntary agency has an opportunity to budget for and plan the services they will offer and provides the local authority with the assurance that certain needs are catered for. We also came across several instances of less formalised partnership arrangements between individual LAs and VAAs and arrangements whereby LAs subscribe to services offered by other agencies.

Service level agreements were used quite widely throughout the sample. However, few of these were concerned with family finding for looked after children, although the less formal partnership arrangements were often in place for potential matching of children and families. Counselling about birth records and help with searching were also frequently contracted out. A number of respondents reported that they routinely contracted out applications for intercountry adoption. They reasoned that they had relatively few applications and thus little opportunity to develop knowledge and skills in this area, and that those experienced in the field were better placed to assess and prepare families for this specific type of adoption. A number of authorities chose to use voluntary organisations and agencies to work with birth families because they thought that birth families may find it hard to work with the agency responsible for their children, especially at the point of placement for adoption. The independence of agencies was therefore valued.

The final area in which there was substantial outsourcing was in post-adoption support. Many local authorities had taken a decision that the most effective means of providing a post-adoption service was to contract out virtually all of it either through SLAs or partnership agreements. The agencies which were commonly being used to provide the services were After Adoption, South West Adoption Network, West Midlands Post Adoption Service, the Post Adoption Centre and Post Adoption Link.

More than one in five local authorities throughout the UK were using After Adoption to provide post-adoption services. Most, but not all, had a full service level agreement, which entitled users to attend training and support groups, to gain access to advice lines and, if needed, to have a one-to-one service. The use of After Adoption was concentrated in the North East and North West of the country and in Wales. At the time of data collection, the first London authorities were signing agreements which would enable the organisation to set up a branch further south.

Seven of the eleven West Midlands authorities that we spoke to subscribed to the West Midlands Post Adoption Service (WMPAS), which offers similar services to those of After Adoption. Five of the 10 South West authorities worked with South West Adoption Network (SWAN).

Pros and cons of contracting out

We have no dedicated post-adoption team. We have thought about it but decided that it was more important to keep up with the family finding and placing of children. We are in the final stages of contracting with After Adoption for post-adoption support. The detail is not yet finalised but they offer a mix of low-level support for all adopters, each given an allocated worker and more intensive services for those who need it. We know we should be providing post-adoption support and we know it is a good recruitment strategy but it is Catch 22!

I think there will be a huge unmet need by making it known that there is this service and I think adopters might get a more consistent and clearer idea of what is on offer (through using a separate agency).

Contracting out post-adoption support 'fills a need to take the load off us. It's not a high enough profile in a busy team, and by outsourcing families get a much better service'.

The next logical leap as I see it will be to have an SLA for group work with individual children. [We] accept, as a principle, that you can't develop those skills "in-house" and even if we did, we are perhaps not the most appropriate people to do it because we don't bring objectivity for the individuals concerned.

For the most part, those who had contracted out the post-adoption services were content with the service received, although there were some reservations concerning the degree of feedback to the commissioning agency. Arguments against contracting out post-adoption support services were that it involved a lack of continuity for families and a lost opportunity for staff to learn from experience, but arguments in favour included greater access for families and a less stigmatising service where families were more in control.

The extent of contracting out for post-adoption services and the implications of this course merits further consideration. We return to this theme later in the discussion section.

The family placement teams

We continue our examination of the provision of support by looking at the family placement teams which are very often the first port of call for adoptive families, especially in the post-placement but pre-order phase. When we spoke to interviewees early in the survey, it became clear that although post-placement and post-adoption support were seen as important tasks, the raison d'être for most teams were their recruitment and family finding activities. Above all, preparation of families was thought to be critical. Even in later interviews, when questions about the relative importance of tasks had been dropped, respondents would spontaneously make statements to this effect.

The main challenge of adoption is preparation. If children are adequately prepared and adopters properly trained, the post-placement challenges are less.

Many authorities were proud of the preparation systems that they had developed. Services that tried to be user friendly in operating at weekends and evenings were commended. Expertise in this area was constantly refined; for example, one respondent spoke about how important she felt it was for FSWs to understand the processes that couples who had received infertility treatment had been through. She organised some sessions for staff from a local self-help organisation.

We have seen in the passages on organisation of services that some authorities were shifting the task of preparation for children. Indeed more than one respondent mentioned that their "Best Value" review had recommended that child preparation was moved to family placement. Another model proposed was group preparation for children.

Although it was by no means the over-riding concern of family placement or adoption units, nevertheless most teams saw themselves (along with CSWs) as providing most of the post-placement support, certainly pre-order, and most respondents thought they were providing at least a reasonably good service. One-third were very proud of their pre-order support provision. A very small minority (just 7 per cent) felt that this aspect of their role was still in development and these tended to be London authorities in hard-pressed areas.

What led to the good service? Respondents felt that the main strengths of the family placement teams lay in the consistency of staffing over time and the sheer experience accrued by staff who had often been working in family placement for several years. The family placement teams were usually described as fairly (41 per cent) or very (56 per cent) stable in terms of membership and staff were considered to be reasonably (37 per cent) or very (60 per cent) experienced in the work in almost all cases. Some staff were new to family placement, but this was usually in the context of joining an established and stable team and coming with a background of social work with children and families.

Training for family placement or adoption workers
While on the topic of knowledge and skills, it is worth mentioning the messages from respondents concerning the training available for family placement staff. On the whole, training was thought to be reasonably well supported by senior management and most authorities have reasonable

budgets to gain access to external courses (very little appropriate training is run "in-house"). Some criticism, however, was levelled at what is generally available. Many felt that while assessment had been fairly well covered, support had been somewhat neglected by external training.

Some felt that many courses were not 'hitting the spot' for workers already enmeshed in adoption practice with many years experience. Opportunities are needed for more in-depth study which allows for the development of skills alongside increased knowledge.

In training around support – not a lot is available and research feedback courses don't allow people to develop their skills.

We need to develop more and then offer training appropriate to the services. No more workshops to talk about 'what will we do?' when there are no answers.

It would be nice to see something come out of the Taskforce on training.

Some are beginning to liaise with other authorities and agencies to acquire the type of training they want by "buying in an American guru" for a day or two. The other, perhaps predictable, criticism is that much of the training tends to be London focused.

Some authorities are sending workers on the more extensive training courses like the "Children in transition" course at the Tavistock Centre. The accredited course in family placement held at Manchester was also mentioned. A number of people also talked about staff attending PQCCA courses (Post Qualifying Child Care Award). However, these were not perceived to be ideal for those working in family placement, being far more focused on child protection and the assessment of risk.

More discussion is clearly needed on an optimum curriculum for adoption support work and on standard setting for practice skills. A number of training packages are available for staff on adoption topics that are produced by independent specialist agencies (e.g. Barnado's and Family Futures). However, these were relatively little mentioned and when they were, it was usually in the context of qualified workers coming new to family placement or adoption work. The omissions seem to apply to experienced staff.

Adoption support services for adoptive families

The general pattern of pre-order support was one of regular contact with families from the family placement worker and, other constraints allowing, visits from the children's worker to ensure that the placement was going well from the child's point of view.

Respondents saw the main tasks in this phase as helping families and children to adjust to each other, assisting them to think about their expectations, and empowering families to parent the child. As time progressed, the task would be to assist in the application for legal adoption. The skills needed here were those of listening, imparting knowledge and helping families to understand what the children may be feeling and what their behaviour may be indicating.

In the early interviews, we spent time talking about post-placement and post-adoption support more freely to explore the needs being perceived, the services that were provided, and how they may be provided. This section was later developed into more structured questions about how particular provision was made in each authority. The topics we questioned on were: ongoing training for adopters, counselling and direct work for adopters and children both pre- and post-order, counselling with regard to searching (Section 51), letterbox arrangements, supporting direct contact, newsletters, support groups for adopters, groups for adoptees and social events. Opportunities were also provided for respondents to tell us about projects that they had in the pipeline.

The way that services were provided across local authorities is illustrated in Table 3. They fall into three broad groups: those which aim to be preventive in terms of offering a point of ongoing contact and opportunities to re-visit areas of need in a timely fashion; services of a more practical nature, like dealing with contact and searching; and finally direct work with families in difficulty after adoption.

Proactive, preventive services

Some form of ongoing training for adopters was available in nearly 80 per cent of authorities. In around half of cases, the FSWs made this provision and in the other half it was shared with or provided in total by another agency. Where another agency was involved, this was often a

Table 3
Means of providing adoption services

Service	Provided in (% of cases)	How provided		
		Fam Pl Team	Shared	Outsourced
Ongoing training	78%	37%	34%	7%
Support groups	63%	36%	9%	18%
Adoptees' groups	26%	5%	5%	16%
Social events	47%	33%	5%	9%
Newsletters	40%	32%	3%	5%
Letterbox	100%	84%	9%	7%
Direct contact	91%	51%	30%	10%
Birth records/searching	100%	67%	24%	9%
Counselling adopters (post order)	100%	48%	33%	19%
Direct work with children (post order)	100%	33%	48%	19%

voluntary organisation or voluntary adoption agency. After Adoption's Parenting Skills course, Adoption UK – *It's a piece of cake*, BAAF (in Scotland), Coram Family and the Post Adoption Centre were also mentioned in this context.

A number of authorities told us of rolling programmes of training for adopters that they had developed. These were mostly run by the family placement staff themselves. The topics frequently dealt with were managing contact with children's birth families, talking about adoption at different stages of children's development, and managing difficult behaviour. One or two authorities would buy in speakers on occasion. One authority taking this course ran four seminars a year, each with a professional speaker. The cost of organising this was shared with neighbouring authorities. Some authorities accessed ongoing training through their service level agreements with voluntary agencies and some would spot-purchase a specific training programme for families that were experiencing particular difficulties.

Support groups for adopters were generally recognised as important, although experiences of running them varied considerably. As is clear from Table 3, just over a third of authorities did not provide a support group. A similar number ran them in-house and the remainder were either shared or outsourced to another agency. Some authorities had thriving groups, which required dividing because they became too large. One respondent told us of a series of groups run in her area, whereby there were two general groups and a social event each year, a series of workshops on specific issues and a further group, known as the attachment group. This latter group ran three or four times a year and aimed to meet the needs of adoptive families that were struggling and needed more intense input.

Several authorities reported a very different experience with trying to establish support groups. They told us of groups that had ceased or failed to get off the ground due to lack of attendance. It was impossible to obtain a feeling for why some were successful and some not. Although some of the agencies that did not have groups were in very remote locations or had very small populations, this was not the general picture. Overall, the agencies with support groups were not different from those without – geographically, administratively or in terms of the number of placements being made. Those reporting successful groups often spoke of adopters' direct involvement in the way the group was run and what topics were dealt with, but then so did some of those in areas that had lost their support groups. It seems likely that adoptive families will differ in the extent to which they wish to continue being so identified or they may wish to attend when they feel a need, rather than commit themselves to regular attendance.

Groups for adopted young people were very thin on the ground. For the most part these groups were provided by the voluntary organisations. After Adoption, the Post Adoption Centre and Adoption UK were all mentioned in this context. One or two respondents discussed some extremely successful groups for children and young people but others had tried to establish such groups with little success. Respondents felt that usually there were not likely to be enough children of similar age and type of need, within any one agency, to form a core group.

The provision of a newsletter was another area in which people were hoping to progress. Many of the authorities that had recently established post-adoption worker posts saw the development of a newsletter as a major task. This relatively low key means of communication was widely seen as a way of keeping doors open and of reminding people that there was help out there should they need it. However, much work and expense are involved in producing attractive and meaningful materials and it might be wasteful to aim for this to be done in every authority.

Overall, however, it seems that these low-key support systems, once in process for some time, bring their own rewards and allow for further development of services. Representatives from authorities with long-standing post-adoption services described it in this way:

> *We've been able to reap the advantage of developing a post-adoption service. There are spin-offs in terms of dedicated volunteers. You can be creative around needs. We have volunteers who are birth mothers, people who are volunteers dealing with admin, and mailings and linking. We are going to start an advisory group – something to pull us together from time to time.*

> *People help with resourcing our annual adopters' workshop and children's events. Adopted adults are very interested in the children's work. As service users, people became aware of the service and offer themselves. It's very labour-intensive though. You have to make sure that you properly register people.*

Arrangements for managing contact and searching

All authorities had some method of dealing with letterbox contact, although on occasion this did seem a little haphazard, with some arrangements remaining with the fieldwork teams and others being managed in family placement. The majority of respondents, however, reported that this task was dealt with in their family placement unit. For some authorities this was a huge administrative task, dealing with as many as 400 exchanges a year. However, respondents were not always happy with the arrangements for managing it. Very few had any monitoring mechanism to ensure that exchanges were made when due, and even fewer had any routine "quality control" ensuring that material exchanged and frequency of exchange were still appropriate to all the parties concerned. There were exceptions where authorities had very established post-adoption sections. Certainly this was to be another task for many of the recently appointed post-adoption workers.

Supporting direct contact was a question that took many of our respondents by surprise. Some respondents felt that, because direct contact arrangements should be made in the best interest of the child, the management of it really ought to be possible between the parties directly and did not see a major role for the agency in most cases. Where there was a need, most of the assistance would be provided by the family placement teams but a substantial role existed for children's social work teams, particularly pre-order. One or two authorities had contracted this aspect of work out to agencies such as Coram Family or the Post Adoption Centre. As contact arrangements become more common, it seems likely that there may be more need for this to become a routine part of post-adoption work. This is certainly firmly embedded in Level 2 of the good practice materials produced by the Adoption and Permanence Taskforce in relation to support services to adoptive families (Department of Health, 2001a). Recent research has addressed both the way in which social work can influence the quality of contact (Neil, 2002) and the areas in which families are likely to need to help (Macaskill, 2002).

Work with families in need after the order

For many authorities, counselling for adopters and direct work for children post order would very much depend on when this need arose and to some extent on the precise nature of the need. Many authorities would continue working with families and children if the need was one that was continuing at the point of order. For needs arising some time after the order, especially if the adoption had happened some time ago, the personal links were often lost and families would have to "re-access" services. For some authorities, this meant that adopters' problems would need to reach the criteria to be recognised as a "child in need". As one respondent stressed:

> They re-access support through CIN area offices. This is not ideal – that's how children came in to start with. It means people access too late.

Increasingly, however, as we saw in the preceding section, in more recent adoptions teams were recognising the need to keep in touch with families and to advertise a post-adoption service, which could act as a first port of call to anyone affected by adoption.

> *One major challenge is how to move to a stage where adopters see the local authority as a resource they can tap into when they need support – before nearly disrupting.*

The tasks of counselling and direct work, however, are in essence difficult to quantify and may lead to relatively long-term work, depending on the problem. We know from the literature reviewed earlier that adoptive families can face difficulties, sometimes substantial, and we know that the rate of disruption of adoptive placements remains relatively high, especially for children placed at older ages. We tried asking in the early interviews about the level of need for services beyond routine visiting. We received varied and quite generalised responses. It was evident that, at a "case" level, staff were thinking about the needs of families but very few seemed to have an overview that would indicate the likely level of demand.

Three major reasons for this were put forward. First, people had been responding to the requests of adoptive families but, perhaps because it was not seen as a core task, had not been relaying this to management.

> *We have been researching the sort of post-adoption support we need. The level of post-adoption work is under-recorded, people almost apologise for doing it.*

Another respondent felt that they did quite well on post-order support but that:

> *It is done through goodwill. If several members of the team left, we would be in trouble in terms particularly of the good relationships they have built with adopters and also their levels of information and expertise.*

The sentiment was frequently expressed that present demands for post-order services may be the tip of the iceberg and that no one really knew just how big the whole might be.

> *It is hard to know what proportion of families need services: we offer a service to anyone who is approved or has had a child placed. More and more are struggling, but services are becoming more visible so more people are coming forward.*

I'd expect more difficulties than there used to be. Looking at the sort of children we are placing these days. There may be learning difficulties or mental health issues or abuse in their histories. We won't know how things will develop.

I would like to write to all our adopters to find out what support services they need but I'm scared that I'll raise expectations that the Department won't be able to deliver.

However, we did hear frequently that families would often leave it very late to try to access services and that by the time they had reached for the telephone they had reached crisis point, which made working with them more difficult and meant that the need for input was immediate. There were also some difficulties in determining what should properly be dealt with by adoption services.

Thinking about teenagers out of control – it is difficult to tease out whether it is anything to do with the adoption or just being teenage.

Frequently respondents felt that they had neither the specific skills nor the time to deal "in house" with some of the more severe difficulties that families presented with. Some brief one-to one work might be offered in some authorities, but anything more than three or four sessions would be detracting from other areas of work. Some authorities had set up contracts with organisations providing post-adoption services, which entitled a certain number of adoptive families to a set amount of one-to-one time, but for others who had no such arrangement, such services would have to be arranged individually for each family in need. In these cases, families would be referred to either the local Child and Adolescent Mental Health Service (CAMHS) or a Child and Family Consultation Service or to an independent organisation or practitioner offering appropriate services. We will deal later with the process of gaining access to these services. For now we will concentrate on other services that were being developed within agencies.

Voluntary adoption agencies – provision of support

Again we have focused until now on itemising the contribution of local authorities, but it is necessary to say a few words about the responses of VAAs in our survey. Overall, the majority of VAAs rated their own performance on both pre-order and post-order support as reasonably or very good, although all recognised areas which required further development. The picture with regard to provision of specific services in the voluntaries was very similar to that of local authorities. A higher proportion (80 per cent) produced newsletters, although in some cases these were produced for a number of types of recipient and not just adoptive families. Slightly more efforts were being made to provide groups or events specifically for children and young people, but this was still true of only 35 per cent. One major difference was in the use of social events for families, which was the case in 90 per cent of agencies. This has long been a feature of many VAAs.

The difference between VAAs and LAs emerged in the degree of conviction expressed by VAA managers as to their ability and willingness to respond to requests for help and the sense that their adopters would return to them if necessary. They were more likely to mention ongoing informal contact after order. Proportionally more of them but by no means all, had already established services like helplines and literature. Perhaps because most were independent and largely autonomous, they felt able to be more responsive to need as it arose. For example, one respondent mentioned that several young people were expressing an interest in searching at a very early age and plans had been made to form a group to work with them together.

Other projects

We were mindful of the fact that local authority workers in the adoption field had recently had to cope with a steep increase of work and that many authorities were still reeling from the restructuring of their teams. Nevertheless, we were interested to know how respondents saw their services developing. Considerable variation existed across authorities in the extent to which they had already developed services. Some had longer histories of focusing on adoption as part of the mainstream of children's services.

For those who had only recently turned their full attention to adoption, the first tasks had to be to find families for children. Most had achieved the mechanisms needed for that part of the task and at the time of data collection were just beginning to address the question of continuing support. As we have seen, many were just emerging from the process of having written action plans, but others had begun to put in place mechanisms to ensure provision and a few had very well established systems. Responses to this area of questioning, therefore, varied tremendously, in both the types of developments and the extent to which plans had been formalised to achieve the aims – or indeed become practice. Some respondents were very non-specific about the ways in which they wished to see the service develop but others had very firm ideas about precise developments which they believed would make a real difference to families.

Some projects were very individual and not necessarily directly related to ongoing support but were nevertheless important achievements and interesting developments. For example, one authority had just successfully reached agreement on a dedicated space for working directly with children. Another spoke of plans to re-introduce group preparation of children who needed adoptive families and yet another described plans to produce a video to help prepare people for direct contact. Events for children were mentioned once or twice, as was a workshop for black and transracially placed children.

Projects that were more to do with appropriate planning of services rather than their actual delivery were also mentioned, thus a couple of authorities talked about inter-agency forums that were being established to expedite service delivery and surveying of adopters to determine what they required from an adoption support service.

A few authorities reported their participation in wider research programmes run in conjunction with universities. The areas being thus investigated included concurrent planning, the impact of a permanence panel and exploring the effect of long-term fostering as opposed to adoption.

The majority of responses to this part of the interview, however, fell into five broad groupings. First, many people spoke of plans to produce informative literature for families and to establish telephone helplines.

For authorities that had contracted out, these services were provided by the various post adoption organisations, but for those who had not, this often formed a major part of their service development. The usual plan was for phone lines to be staffed by family placement, adoption or sometimes post adoption specialists, for set hours in the week, with a monitored answering service outside of those hours. One authority reported 24-hour telephone cover.

The further development of ongoing training opportunities and support groups for adopters was also high on the agenda for many respondents. Sometimes they envisaged this being achieved through their own efforts, sometimes through their consortium, and sometimes by means of buying in an appropriate parenting skills course.

Another popular service was that of mentoring or "buddying", a practice whereby experienced adopters volunteer to be available for others who are just starting out on the adoption journey. This offers people the chance to speak to someone who has probably been through similar trials rather than having to talk to a professional. These arrangements were perceived to be extremely helpful for adopters and, if not already in place, were on the development list of several authorities.

Of all the projects discussed by respondents, the area most frequently mentioned was that of improving access to therapeutic and educational support (an area we shall discuss further later). On occasion, this was mentioned more as a recognition that it was an area that needed addressing, but in other cases teams were in the process of making representations to augment the remit of existing multi-disciplinary teams in the locality to include adoptive families. In a few cases, plans were afoot to organise dedicated services, which could be available in-house for adopters. In the case of therapeutic help, these were usually regular "surgeries" organised by a psychologist, counsellor or play therapist. In other cases, people were planning or had already established a service level agreement with an appropriate resource to ensure that families had access to help when it was needed.

Respite care came up relatively rarely among local authority respondents but was thought of as significant for some adoptive placements. While respite care could be available through the Children in Need arrangements, some of those we spoke to felt that this was not necessarily appropriate. They thought that something was needed that could be more flexible and perhaps less like returning to care. They were looking at respite for adopters by adopters, taking on board the differences between adoptive families and fostering arrangements, but also respite care that did not necessarily mean the child leaving home, but which would give the parties some space from each other. There was also a recognition that respite must be in the interests of the child as well as the adopters.

We saw from the literature review that VAAs have been heavily represented in innovative practice development in the past. Indeed their preparedness to report and share their experience can be seen as a significant driving force in the present developments in adoption practice. When it came to asking about current projects and developments, this broader perspective, innovative attitude and ability to adapt and respond were again in evidence.

In comparison with local authorities, proportionally many more VAAs were involved in structured research projects. Thus, a couple of agencies described their involvement in investigating the feasibility and effects of true concurrent planning for children. Others spoke of trials relating to assessing attachment styles of children and families and how this related to the manner in which placements progressed.

Respondents from VAAs were also more likely to talk about services for children and young people, and indeed to include them in consultation and planning regarding services. Two respondents described the development of a website for the dissemination of information, to both professionals and users. The perception was that this was likely to become a major route for initial help-seeking, especially for young people. Plans for developing appropriate respite services were in place in nearly a quarter of VAAs and projects addressing the specific needs of black and minority ethnic families were mentioned on three occasions.

One of the major features of many of the VAA projects was in dissemination and fine honing of developments. This is possibly, in part at least, due to the way in which VAAs are funded. Although they may have access to grants to research a response to an area of need, it is ultimately necessary for them to "sell" their services to realise income. Some VAAs we spoke to were highly developed in this regard and were involved in the production of parenting skills programmes for adopters and were offering a range of other services for families which local authorities may buy into. A service to local authorities offering advice and consultation on establishing appropriate support services was also described.

Although this sort of development tended to be more evident among VAAs, it did not apply to all of those who participated; neither was it entirely absent among local authorities. As we have said elsewhere, there were examples of extremely good practice in some LAs, although there was less imperative to develop services into transportable packages.

Summary

- The majority of authorities reported that they had only just caught up with the imperatives of improved planning and decision making: family placement teams had been concentrating on improving their recruitment and preparation arrangements and were just beginning to turn their attention to the development of support services.
- That said, most authorities were making provision for the majority of commonly recognised adoption support tasks. However, in most cases these arrangements continued to be reactive rather than proactive, with widespread recognition that these services could be better organised and delivered.
- Pre-order support from the local authority was felt to be managed at least reasonably well in over 90 per cent of cases. However, this proportion dropped to just over 40 per cent when looking at support that continued after the order.
- Although cases were not generally kept actively open after the order, almost all authorities said that they had long had an "open door" policy. But it was increasingly recognised that it was necessary to "hold the door open" by such means as newsletters, ongoing training and support groups for adopters as well as services for adopted young people. The latter were less well developed.
- Almost 40 per cent of authorities had, or were about to have, post-adoption teams; just under 10 per cent had well-established post-adoption teams and the services provided by them were very similar to those traditionally associated with VAAs. They typically had full

literature on their services available for adoptive families, ran support groups and had newsletters.

- In many of the authorities the provision of support services was shared with other agencies and contracting out of post-adoption services was common. This tended to be concentrated in the regions where established specialist providers were available.

- Representatives recognised both positives and negatives in contracting out. Arguments in favour included offering choice, independence from social services, more coherent and comprehensive services, economy of scale, allowing teams to concentrate on the core tasks of recruitment assessment and family finding. Arguments against included worries about lack of continuity for families, loss of skills in family placement teams, uncertainty about the quality of service being provided, and loss of experience of the progress of placements that could feed into better preparation.

- Projects being developed within local authorities were mostly concerned with the establishment of post-adoption worker posts, the setting up of support groups or re-vamping the letterbox contact system and organising written information for users about support services. Organising appropriate training for children's social workers was also high on the agenda for many. Authorities that were already more organised were beginning to turn their attention to more elaborate developments such as appropriate respite care for adoptive placements. Some were beginning to work on concurrent planning and others were working on arrangements to provide dedicated teams with the skills needed to offer therapeutic and counselling work to adoptive families. One or two mentioned groups for adopted children and young people.

- The major differences between local authority and voluntary adoption agencies were, first, in the use of regular social events and other informal mechanisms for keeping in touch with families; and second, in the degree of confidence expressed in their ability to respond effectively, although not necessarily from within their own resources, to a family's needs.

- In terms of specific service developments to support families, VAAs were proportionally more likely to mention existing arrangements or plans for the more elaborate support services, such as appropriate respite care or support groups for specific groups of parents or children.

- The traditional role of some VAAs in consolidating and disseminating available knowledge was observed in their enthusiasm to instigate and participate in research, in their development of services in response to emerging needs, and in their willingness to utilise new technologies such as the internet.

Links across agencies and disciplines

The use and function of consortia

Almost all of the LAs we spoke to were members of a consortium, and on the whole, these were viewed positively. some consortia were relatively new and just beginning to get a grip on what the various members hoped to achieve through them. Some of the more established consortia offered substantial opportunities for shared training of both adopters and staff, for sharing support groups and other support activities as well as their intended function of sharing families for children. Indeed one consortium member responded:

Oh no, we've given up on sharing families – that was too com-plicated . . . but it is tremendously valuable as an opportunity to share practice development ideas.

Questions arose as to what consortia were for and how they were supposed to work. Many respondents discussed the problems encountered in trying to share families when there were net consumers and net providers. For example, a large city may put forward the names of many children but very few families, while their more rural neighbours may be offering the opposite. Indeed, more than one respondent reported that as a large city authority they were not welcome as full members of their local consortium because 'we're too hungry!' A variety of mechanisms were being tried to overcome these problems such as setting a ceiling on the number of "free" families or "reduced-price" families. (In the UK, the agency that recruits and prepares an adoptive family is entitled to a fee in the event that the child placed with them is from a different agency. These fees are known as inter-agency fees. In a consortium arrangement the inter-agency fee may be reduced or dispensed with altogether.)

One effect of consortia was to reveal differences in practice between authorities, so many were working towards a more uniform type of practice in order for some family placement functions such as preparation to be shared. Another effect was the exclusion of voluntary agencies in many areas. Some consortia were setting up various offshoots of the placement sharing function, which was leading to managers at different levels needing to attend a wide variety of meetings. One might question whether such a plethora of forums for the discussion and development of practice is appropriate. These issues were particularly apparent in areas in which other practice groups were also active, for example, BAAF regional groups. Those whose consortia had not yet moved into policy development and practice sharing were often anxious that it did so.

Several of the regional post-adoption services were related to consortia also, although not all consortia members necessarily subscribed to the services offered. Many wanted to see more adoption work being undertaken at regional level. For example, some respondents in areas with relatively high minority ethnic populations felt that specific preparation groups could be organised on a regional basis.

As mentioned, voluntary adoption agencies were often excluded from local authority consortia, although this was not always the case. However, where there were also regional practice groups they were welcome members. Additionally they had access to the Consortium of Voluntary Adoption Agencies, which also provided much appreciated opportunities for sharing.

Education services

Some variation was apparent among respondents as to the importance of education with regard to adopted children, although most were in agreement that the educational needs of *looked after* children should be prioritised. Some felt, very keenly, that adopted children got a poor response from education services and that there should be some avenue for fast-tracking services. Others felt that, once adopted, it was appropriate that children were treated as any other child, although this sentiment was sometimes followed by the corollary that services should be generally more available to all children.

For some respondents, education was not perceived as an area in which families often faced problems. Sometimes, of course the children were pre-school at placement. However, even though children may be being placed at a young age, this should not be taken to mean that difficulties may not emerge at a later stage. The comments made about the histories of the youngsters being placed and the fact that Rushton *et al* (1988) found that concerns about school took on more importance as time passed, ought to suggest a longer-term perspective and one that anticipates a potential need for support.

Some general issues were mentioned frequently with regard to education. One, which might be fairly simply remedied with appropriate training, was the perennial problem of standard teaching practice exploring areas of great sensitivity to children who cannot gain access to information about their own histories, for example, how much you weighed at birth or what colour your eyes were.

The other problem was predictably the need to ensure that appropriate provisions were made for children who needed extra support at school. Two strands emerged: first, the financial matters which came to the fore particularly when placements were made across administrative boundaries and, second, problems with the geographical location of suitable schools.

In line with government guidance, almost all authorities reported having some form of liaison with education, all had designated teachers with a special remit for looked after children. Some had educational representation within multi-disciplinary teams within children's services. Critically these services were often not available to children after adoption unless they reached the criteria for services as a child in need. One respondent answered our question about liaison with education thus:

> *Oh what a disaster – two years ago we, the adoption team, really got to grips with this and we had our own education liaison person – fantastic! As soon the LA got their system set up we lost him . . . Now there is **nothing** specific once the adoption order has gone through.*

Some voluntary agencies had forged links with education specialists who were able to offer advice and consultation to families or workers, and in some cases undertook a degree of liaison on their behalf.

Therapeutic services for children and families

Very few agencies (VAAs or SSDs) had specialist workers on their teams who could undertake specific intervention work with children or families, though most had workers experienced in generalised support and/or direct work with children. However, this was usually seen as a skill level that would be appropriate for updating children's understanding of their situation, rather than approaching a therapeutic task.

We asked whether it may be beneficial to have family placement staff specifically trained in therapeutic techniques to assist families in difficulty. Broadly speaking, about half the sample felt that this might be helpful in terms of being able to offer a speedy response to some families at least. But some had reservations about the demand on resources, the time taken for training and to do the work, and the distraction from other core functions of teams. If this was an additional resource for the existing team it would be more acceptable. Those who were less enthusiastic felt that there was a potential for role conflict, saying that social workers and therapists are different. They felt that social workers should do what they do well: that is to identify a problem and know what to do next. Some people also felt that families want or need independence from social services, and that being referred to a specialist can be helpful in itself.

In response to our question about ease of access to other services, the almost universal immediate response was 'very difficult'. It transpired from talking further that they were usually able to locate and eventually gain access to some appropriate service for people, but the process could be time-consuming, expensive and often involve a considerable amount of travelling for families. The exceptions to this were those few authorities which had access to multi-disciplinary teams based either in social services departments or health authorities, or those based in major cities that had specialist centres. Some local authorities and most of the voluntary adoption agencies kept records of individuals with whom they had worked and who they knew were able to offer appropriate interventions for adoptive families. Agencies based in London would list a series of specialist units whose services they had found excellent.

The main point of referral for families in difficulty in most authorities was Child and Adolescent Mental Health Services (CAMHS). These services have been much criticised in the past and are already under scrutiny and reform in their own right. The respondents in this survey generally expressed disappointment in the services provided from the point of view of the needs of placed and adopted children. CAMHS units were perceived to be over-stretched, under-resourced and to have experienced difficulty in recruitment and retention of staff. These factors led to long waiting lists; in some areas periods of eight months were not uncommon. The waiting problems were felt to be particularly important in the context of adoption. Additional to this, dismay was expressed about the lack of priority given to adopted children and the lack of understanding of the specific features of adoption. Many respondents felt that there persisted, in many CAMHS units, a culture of anticipating a "dysfunctional family".

In total, around two-thirds of those respondents who were specifically questioned on this topic reported significant waiting problems with CAMHS. Around three-quarters felt there were difficulties with the needs of adoptive families meeting CAMHS criteria. Adoption was not often perceived to be seen as a priority for CAMHS units and often the service offered was not thought to be entirely appropriate. In the words of one respondent:

> *I am told there are experienced people there and they would probably deal well with general issues around relationships. But if they concern adoption I would feel that Post Adoption Centres are more appropriate for this as they are experienced whereas CAMHS may not be so up to date.*

Some exceptions to this generally unhappy picture were noted, however. A minority of respondents reported excellent relationships with and experiences of CAMH services in their areas. Again we return perhaps to the importance of senior personnel. Certainly it was the view of one interviewee that the manager of her local CAMHS unit understood the problems of children in transition and those in placement and was active in developing appropriate services. Several others made comments to the effect that 'you only need one person in CAMHS with an interest in looked after or adopted children [for the service to be enhanced]'. One authority told us how they abandoned negotiations for a multi-disciplinary team for adoptive families with their local CAMHS unit but succeeded easily with a unit in a neighbouring NHS Trust. This experience suggests that the manner in which CAMH services are provided may be more to do with the professional interests of personnel than responding to community needs.

We documented in the literature review the emergence of specialist adoption centres. Services like Keys Attachment Centre, the Post Adoption Centre, Brighton and Hove Attachment Centre and Family Futures were mentioned frequently and were often the preferred avenue if finance permitted. The specialist units at Great Ormond Street, and The Maudsley Hospitals along with the Tavistock Clinic were also popular – especially for London-based authorities, although on occasion geography and catchment areas were a problem.

Around 20 per cent of authorities reported some kind of multi-disciplinary team within the social services department that they could refer to. These were exciting new developments taking place in the context of "joining-up" services and improving provision for looked after children. We shall look at these in more detail in the next section.

Because of the difficulty of gaining access to external therapeutic resources for adoptive families, a few authorities had set up links with, and procured the funding for, a psychologist or similar consultant to be available to adopters on a surgery basis. One of the providers we spoke to was offering one day a fortnight to anyone who wanted some time. Much of her work was one-off consultation, and she did not become involved in working with children directly, but would see people for three or four sessions if needed.

Although VAAs also tried to engage with mainstream provision, this was not always easy to achieve as they may need to negotiate with many different areas; this was particularly true in London. Many had therefore organised direct links with appropriately qualified psychologists and therapists whom they could call on for staff consultation or direct work as and when needed.

Joining up services

One of the major thrusts of government guidance in relation to looked after children in particular has been the need for health, education and social services collectively to own their corporate parenting responsibilities. The evidence from this survey is that this is beginning to happen. Most authorities had achieved means of fast tracking looked after children through CAMHS units generally. Additionally, we were advised of a number of projects comprising multi-disciplinary teams engaged on the task of easing the difficulties faced by, and presented by, looked after children in school and in the community at large. These were variously located in both health and social services. Most of these teams were to be found in England and many had emerged as a result of the Quality Protects (QP) initiative using QP funding. Some authorities had multi-disciplinary teams that had been in existence prior to Quality Protects. These were often based in other areas of the social services department, for example, youth services.

In one authority the arrangement was described thus:

Within CAMHS there is a full-time psychologist post for LAC/ adopters. This is divided into two part-time psychologist posts. The psychologists will see families if they need help with management strategies. But if the child needs support then they will fast-track them into CAMHS.

The major issue, from the point of view of this survey, is that many of these projects were tightly defined in relation to the families and children that they could work with. Many were services for *looked after* children. It may be possible to negotiate their working with adoptive families, but strictly speaking such families fell outside their remit once the order had been granted. Other teams that might be able to offer the necessary knowledge and skill were sometimes to be found in children's social services under titles such as Family Support Team. However, in these cases families would have to be classified as having "children in need". This raises other concerns from the point of view of an adoptive family. The majority of respondents in our sample felt that adopted children should be seen as a priority for therapeutic services, mainly because of their histories and the fact that disruption may well be the likely outcome if help were not available. However, some felt that on principle this help should be available equally to all who needed it and others felt that looked after children should be the higher priority.

Thinking further as to how services should develop, respondents felt that a range of intervention agencies was appropriate so that people could choose what they felt was most likely to be helpful to them. A multi-disciplinary approach was felt to be essential and a preference was evident for independence from social services. One or two mentioned the possibility of developing regional centres providing a variety of interventions and support.

Overall there was an impression that our respondents, with some exceptions, felt that CAMHS and education personnel, at both management and practitioner level, were poorly informed about adoption. One or two were generous enough to suggest that social workers could probably be better informed about the work of the other two services too. However, little mention was made of joint training across disciplines that might encourage greater levels of understanding on all sides. One or two initiatives had been developed like producing leaflets designed to inform teachers about what adoption may mean for a child, and in one instance, an attempt was made to arrange a joint seminar for exchange of knowledge and information across disciplines.

Crossing boundaries

A substantial number of adoptive placements are already made across administrative boundaries. With regard to support this raises issues of not knowing the availability of local resources.

> *The other challenge is long-distance placements. Children are resilient about cultural and geographical adaptations but trying to organise resources when you don't know what is available and there is resistance from the other area is very difficult. This is likely to get worse with the National Register.*

While an ability to respond locally to local need is to be admired, much more clarity is required about what local areas provide. With the plethora of projects and organisations now offering the potential to support families in difficulty, we were interested to know how authorities kept track of the services available. Most had no structured means of doing so. They learned of services by word of mouth or from leaflets that arrived in the mail. It may be that this should be a responsibility of information officers within councils, and indeed some authorities did produce directories.

However, as highlighted by one VAA director, there is a danger of over-load. The document she received was so comprehensive, including services for a wide variety of users, and so regularly updated, that neither she nor her staff had the time to digest it. There is perhaps room for a regional response here, possibly through consortia activity, to catalogue and update adoption relevant services in the area, including independent practitioners, in a form that could be accessible to professionals (and users) from other parts of the country. Another respondent told us of a project her agency was currently involved in to develop a website, which she hoped would act as a database for families and staff to identify resources. However, this was still in its early stages. This seems potentially a valuable way forward, but to be truly useful will require sufficient detail and accuracy of description and will depend upon reliable and regular updating.

The other major "cross-boundary" issue is the perennial problem of funding support needs that arise in these circumstances. Respondents held a variety of opinions concerning how funding should be organised, but spoke with one voice on the importance of it being clarified one way or another in order for delay and uncertainty to be reduced.

Monitoring the views of users

Most authorities do not monitor adopters' views routinely, although they survey all other carers. They rely instead on feedback provided in support groups or via social worker visits. Some have had some feedback in the context of Best Value or SSI inspections. In the light of previous surveys indicating users' difficulty in making contact with appropriate services or obtaining what they really want, this is disappointing. That said, it was a task that was on the drawing board for most authorities. A few authorities are beginning to survey their adopters at the point of the adoption hearing and some had agreements with adopters as to their willingness to be contacted and to provide feedback. One authority was in the process of having an independent team survey adopted children. Although there was relatively little monitoring of views, a number of respondents mentioned that adopters (and on occasion adopted young people) participated in service planning and sometimes in service delivery too. This is to be welcomed. Bearing in mind the discussion about user satisfaction in the literature review and the fact that this area is currently so under-developed, it might be helpful if something were to be produced from the Taskforce on this topic.

Services for families of minority ethnicity

As we saw earlier, when we looked at the profile of children placed for adoption, a wide variation existed between authorities in the proportion of children who were of minority ethnic background. Over one-third of authorities placed no such children in our year of interest and in a further third, black children accounted for less than 10 per cent of placements made. For a few authorities, over half the children placed were of minority ethnicity. Clearly the importance of a service attuned to the needs of black families and children will vary according to the proportion of work that is needed.

Relatively little was said about ethnicity, beyond the almost universal experience of black and dual heritage children having to wait longer for placement. One person mentioned her concern that fewer black children were referred for placement than she would expect from the proportion of looked after children who were of minority ethnic heritage. Some teams were pleased with the fact that they had managed to recruit black and Asian social workers to work with minority ethnic families in their communities. Others bemoaned the difficulties of recruitment. A few people mentioned preparation groups for non-English-speaking applicants. These were not surprisingly concentrated in agencies with a high minority ethnic population, but they were also agencies located in the Midlands and the north of England. The lack of mention of this in London and the south was somewhat surprising. It seems likely that this is due to the fact that these groups were usually organised through consortia and those in the north tend to be longer established and thus further down the line in terms of sharing and development.

Some of the VAAs spoke of projects that they were involved in that were providing services for black and minority ethnic families. One was a black families project which has been running for three years. A plan to organise a London-wide support group for black adopters was mentioned, although this was still in the early stages.

In the literature review we identified very little research that helps us to understand the experience of black and minority ethnic adoptive families. However, we have also seen that agencies are only just beginning to turn their attention to monitoring of adopters' views in general. It is to be hoped that consideration of users' cultural and ethnic backgrounds will be taken into account when this gets underway. It is clearly an area that also needs more specific research, to determine if and how needs might differ from those of other adopters.

Burning issues

Finally, a couple of issues that so concerned all our early interviewees that we included questions on them in the main survey, although they were not directly to do with availability of support services. The first of these was *adoption allowances*. The feedback from the survey is that it is absolutely critical that solutions are found. The disparity between authorities and areas leads to considerable difficulties. Most feel that families should not be means tested, that there should be a national formula which takes account of the likely needs of individual children and that is fairly distributed, and that the way it is worked out is transparent. Some have suggested that it should be paid like child benefit.

Who pays for therapeutic or other support services after adoption was likewise a major topic for many of our respondents. The delays that can be caused while arguments ensue between various departments of the same authority (education, health and social services) or between different local authorities can be disastrous. Although some managers expressed one preference or the other, the impression is that most managers just want a rapid resolution to the problems.

What we didn't ask about

The topics that respondents raised at the end of the interview which were important to them but not covered by us concerned *contact arrangements, court systems, and services for birth parents*. These were strictly speaking outside of our remit, since we were focusing on services for adoptive families, but we take the point that these are important to the success of adoptive placements.

Regional variations

Where we have noted regional variations in the course of the analysis, we have commented on them in the relevant sections of text. On the whole, rather less variation was found than anticipated. Scotland and Northern Ireland operate rather differently to England and Wales in terms of their structures and management, the children and families social work coming under the auspices of the health service in Northern Ireland, and both countries having their own governance. Authorities in these countries have not been subject to quite the same array of government directives as in England and Wales, but reports and consultation documents have been issued in these countries which are broadcasting similar messages. Overall, the respondents we spoke to appeared just as aware of the need to both improve their own services and forge effective links with other providers.

The representatives we spoke to gave the impression of services developing rapidly. Gaining access to services seemed to be similarly difficult, with the exception of a small number of central city locations or areas in which there happened to be specific provision.

In some of the more rural and remote areas, where people may have to travel some distance to access services, this was not seen as a particular problem. People in those areas generally have to travel to achieve most things, even to buy a washing machine. However, when looking at very isolated authorities, such as in Scotland or the Channel Islands, severe difficulties can be experienced because of the lack of local resources generally.

Summary

- Adoption consortia were widely established, although some difficulties exist in achieving equity across members with different levels of need. As forums for sharing ideas, experiences and developing practice, they were almost universally appreciated.
- Many consortia were beginning to share such tasks as preparation groups and ongoing training for adopters and training for staff. Such moves were usually seen positively and were on the wish list for those whose consortium had not yet taken such steps.

- Voluntary agencies were sometimes excluded from local authority adoption consortia although they usually belonged to other similar organisations.
- The majority of local authorities reported improvements in liaison with education services for looked after children although most commented that there was further to go.
- In only a minority of cases did the mechanisms in place for the education of looked after children extend to adopted children. Although the majority felt that children should continue to benefit from these schemes after the order was granted, opinion was somewhat divided on this point.
- For families that needed a greater degree of intervention than was available from the family placement team, all authorities had access to CAMHS (or similar).
- The experience of CAMH services was mixed, but the majority reported ongoing difficulties with waiting lists and problems of eligibility of the types of problem families presented with, and sometimes with the inappropriateness of the approach taken by CAMHS personnel.
- Examples were given of newly established multi-disciplinary teams based in either CAMHS or social services departments providing services for looked after children and their carers, but these only occasionally had a specific remit to respond to the needs of adoptive families.
- Most respondents reported that they were usually able to locate an appropriate source of additional support, but the process of doing so was often extremely time-consuming and could be expensive and may entail families travelling long distances.
- A need was identified to improve the understanding of adoption among both managers and practitioners in education and children's mental health services. Some authorities and organisations were beginning to produce literature for schools but evidence of inter-disciplinary training was sparse.
- No pattern was discernible in those authorities that had developed good inter-agency relationships. The indications from the interviews were that obstacles could be either in senior management at a strategic

planning level, or at the level of individual schools or clinics. The critical point seemed to be to have someone within the other service with an interest in adoption.

- The practice of placing children beyond the boundaries of the placing authority raises a host of difficulties to do with knowledge of services and funding. Both of these need addressing.
- Very few local authorities had arrangements in place to elicit routine feedback from service users and only one respondent mentioned plans to survey children's views.
- Relatively little was said about services for families and children of minority ethnic background.

8 Discussion and conclusions

Numerous developments have taken place to lay more appropriate foundations to the service provided by local authorities. In the best prepared authorities, the adoption support on offer compares favourably with, and outclasses that provided by some VAAs. The process of identification of children needing adoption and procedures for securing adoptive homes for them seems to have been tightened up considerably. The moves towards specialisation in children's teams and in family placement seem likely to be beneficial for children. Work is beginning on developing post-placement and post-adoption services. Areas of work that are within the remit and the skill base of social workers are being attended to, or at least there are plans to do so. The evidence from the survey is that social services departments are responding to their area of responsibility with regard to adoptive families as far as they are able, but when difficulties appear, adoptive families need to have access to services provided by other disciplines. It is less evident that the relevant mainstream services in health and education have as yet responded as effectively.

At this point we intend to bring together, much more than previously, the findings from the two parts of this project. We therefore approach the discussion in a slightly different manner to what has gone before. We have provided summaries at the end of each section of the text which highlight the major findings and our intention is to concentrate here on three critical points which need further exploration. In our view, the important issues that have emerged as a result of the study, relate to three fundamental aspects of support: the first is assessment of need and planning service provision; the second is service delivery mechanisms; and the third is the effectiveness of services and interventions.

Assessment of need and planning service provision

It seems to us that a good deal of attention is paid to the needs of individual children and their families, particularly prior to placement. This of course occurs because of the importance of anticipating potential support needs in relation to adoption allowances, as well as needing this information to effect a suitable match between prospective adopters and waiting children. However, it appears to be done solely on a case-by-case basis. Aggregate data are lacking concerning the likely levels of difficulty that children may present. Many respondents in the early interviews were unable to tell us the proportion of children placed who had emotional or behavioural problems and estimates of the proportion of cases that might need services beyond routine social work support were very difficult to extract. It is true that some difficulties tend to emerge as a result of a mismatch between parental management style and children's difficulties. However, it would seem essential for managers to have an overview of the likely level of problems in order that appropriate arrangements may be made to provide services.

From the literature review we know a little of what adopters say they find most challenging and we have some information as to how many children this might affect. But it is only on the basis of much improved record keeping that it will be possible to judge the likely training needs of adopters and staff or the level of expertise required to help.

We have seen that respondents report that people often approach services too late, waiting until the family is in crisis. The moves towards keeping in touch with families will hopefully encourage adopters (or their children) to come forward earlier but it will still be necessary to assess families' needs and make a decision about the best course of action. In our early interviews we asked whether family workers used any structured format for the assessment of need, having in mind the Framework for the Assessment of Children in Need (Department of Health, 1999). At the time of data collection no structured assessment appeared to be used. These specialist practitioners relied on their knowledge and understanding of adoption to assess and advise on possible courses of action. The Framework referred to is presented in the consultation paper, *Providing Effective Adoption Support* (Department of Health, 2002b) and it is clearly the intention that this should in future be used for assessment of adoption support needs. In its current format it is not designed for children in transition, nor is it geared to families forming new relationships, but a modified version might produce a more standardised method of assessment: one that could potentially be used to enhance the quality of aggregate record keeping.

Delivery of adoption support services

Several issues concerning delivery of services were thrown up in the course of the project. One of the most pressing concerns is how the recent suggestion from the Department of Health that the boundaries between post-placement and post-adoption should be made less of, fits with the recent establishment of a number of *post-adoption* posts and indeed with the contracting out arrangements. It remains to be seen whether this suggestion, currently in the consultation phase, will be taken up, and if so, how it will be interpreted and embraced in practice.

A second major issue about delivery of services is that of geography. We did not start out with any strong views about regional delivery of services but several features of the survey findings suggest that this may be the way for adoption services to develop in future. It was clear from the survey findings that, although local authority adoption agencies continue to operate largely independently, evidence of shared practice is increasing, particularly so in relation to certain elements of support. The sharing of services is leading to a need to review and revise policy and practice guidance to produce consistency across authorities that are working together. Authorities themselves recognise duplication in their work, sometimes costly duplication, as in the case of advertising for recruitment and family finding. Although larger authorities place many children and develop more substantial skills, those that deal with smaller numbers have less opportunity to learn from experience and it is less cost-effective for them to develop the low-level supports that were thought to be so important, like support groups and newsletters. Indeed, a number of the smaller authorities have recognised this and it is a major factor in their decision to contract out post-adoption services, which in effect is already offering regionally based services, albeit with outreach surgeries and outposts.

One or two of our respondents also mentioned the desirability of regional "one-stop shops" in terms of adoption support. Such a move would of course address the inequity of distribution of specialist services across the UK but it would also represent a fairly dramatic reform of the existing structures.

In moving on to thinking about services for adoptions in difficulty, we saw that in some cases, although we know not what proportion, the skills and available time of family placement workers were insufficient to address problems experienced by families and referral to an alternative service would be seen as the option of choice. A number of concerns were raised in relation to this. First, access was difficult to what ought to be universally available services. CAMHS in particular was criticised for the length of waiting lists, the eligibility of diagnoses, and appropriateness of services. Sometimes these issues were addressed by the new multi-disciplinary teams, but often not. Their remit was usually the welfare of looked after children. Those teams that were based in children's social services often required that a family's need met the "children in need" criteria. This is neither highly likely nor helpful in the context of adoption. Evaluations and reports of specialist projects, as far as they exist, stress the importance of the joint focus of practitioners, from different disciplines, on the special aspects of the adoptive experience.

In the current environment we take the view that we ought to be aiming for the presence of a specialist service in each region. We heard examples of people from Scotland accessing a London based service because that was what was considered likely to be helpful! However, in their recent consultation document, the Department of Health emphasise the importance of facilitating adoptive families' access to mainstream services (Department of Health, 2002b). If this is to happen, it seems that a considerable task lies ahead with the aim of firstly persuading mental health service providers of the need for assistance in adoptive placements, and secondly in effectively encouraging an adoption perspective in their work with families.

Currently the special role traditionally associated with voluntary adoption agencies appears to be hanging in the balance. The continued existence of VAAs relies on their developing services which local authorities are prepared to purchase. These services have traditionally been mainly concerned with recruitment and preparation of prospective adopters and then providing a high-quality support service after placement and beyond the order. With much encouragement and some facilitation (in the guise of special funds) local authority adoption agencies are now developing rapidly. They typically report on highly active recruitment work and the improvement of preparation and support services. The challenge may well be for VAAs to identify other areas of work for which they are ideally suited. Indications of this are already beginning to appear with some VAAs offering such services as birth parent counselling and contact mediation.

Effectiveness

The aspect we have not yet touched on is effectiveness. The literature review revealed that, of all the specialist service developments, very few have been evaluated. We do not know, even in terms of relatively routine services, what elements of a service are valued or what elements make a difference. With very few exceptions the picture is similar with regard to specialist interventions. Survey respondents had reservations in some cases about the lack of feedback from intervention services, and uncertainty about what interventions were taking place with a family or child. Although some respondents had had substantial experience with referrals to specialist agencies and were confident in referring families to them, others were either vague when we asked about effectiveness or they stated their ignorance openly. The impression gained from discussions with some survey respondents was largely one of "refer and hope". We were told of cases where families had received every conceivable type of service but that nothing had helped. A minority of placements will inevitably fail, but it is crucial to learn more about what works, for whom, and in what circumstances.

Conclusions

Research-based knowledge on the effectiveness of adoption support, and knowledge of the means of providing services more equitably are both important. Few benefits will accrue to adoptive families if the delivery system improves greatly but if the interventions are mis-targeted, or inexpertly delivered. Few benefits will accrue to families if the effectiveness of certain interventions has been established but they are not equitably distributed.

References

Adoption UK (2000) *It's a piece of cake? A new parent support programme developed by adopters for adopters*, Daventry: Adoption UK.

Ainsworth M M and Blehar *et al* (1978) *Patterns of Attachment: A psychological study of the strange situation*, Hillsdale: NJ, Erlbaum.

Argent H (ed) (1987) *Keeping the Doors Open: A review of post-adoption services*, London: BAAF.

BAAF (2002) *Placing Children First: A five-year strategy 2002/7*, London: BAAF.

Banks N (1992a) 'Some considerations of "racial" identification and self-esteem when working with mixed ethnicity children and their mothers as social service clients', *Social Services Research* 3, pp 32–41.

Banks N (1992b) 'Techniques for direct identity work with black children', *Adoption & Fostering* 16:3, pp 19–25.

Barth R and Berry M (1988) *Adoption and Disruption: Rates, risks and responses*, NY: Aldine de Gruyter.

Barth R P and Miller J M (2000) 'Building effective post-adoption services: what is the empirical foundation?', *Family Relations* 49:4, pp 447–55.

Beek M (1999) 'Parenting children with attachment difficulties: views of adoptive parents and implications for post-adoption support', *Adoption & Fostering* 23:1, pp 16–23.

Bondy D (1997) *The Effectiveness of Brief Family Therapy with Families Adopting Special Needs Children*, New York University School of Social Work.

Borland M, O'Hara G and Triseliotis J (1991a) 'Placement outcomes for children with special needs', *Adoption & Fostering* 15:2, pp 18–28.

Borland M, O'Hara G and Triseliotis J (1991b) *Permanency Planning and Disruptions in the Lothian Region*, Edinburgh, Scotland: University of Edinburgh, Department of Social Policy and Social Work/Scottish Office, Central Research Unit Papers.

Boston M and Szur R (1983) *Psychotherapy with Severely Deprived Children*, London: Routledge and Kegan Paul.

Bretherton I (1987) *New Perspectives on Attachment Relations: Security, communication and internal working models*, Chichester: Wiley.

Burnell A and Briggs A (1997a) 'The next generation of post-placement and post adoption services: a complementary contract approach', *Adoption & Fostering* 19:3, pp 6–10.

Burnell A and Briggs A (1997b) 'Partnership in post-adoption services: evaluating the first year of a complementary contract', *Adoption & Fostering* 21:3, pp 50–56.

Cicchetti D and Toth S (1995) 'A developmental psychopathology perspective on child abuse and neglect', *Journal of the American Academy of Child & Adolescent Psychiatry* 34, pp 541–65.

Clark H B, Prange M E, Lee B, Boyd L A, McDonald B A and Stewart E S (1994) 'Improving adjustment outcomes for foster children with emotional and behavioural disorders: Early findings from a controlled study on individualised services', *Journal of Emotional and Behavioral Disorders* 2, pp 207–18.

Cline F (1992) *Hope for High Risk and Rage-filled Children*, Evergreen, Colorado: Foster W Cline.

Cohen N J, Coyne J and Duvall J (1993) 'Adopted and biological children in the clinic: family, parental and child characteristics', *Journal of Child Psychology and Psychiatry* 4, pp 545–62.

Cooper H (1998) *Synthesizing Research: A guide for literature reviews*, London: SAGE Publications.

Cordell A, Nathan C and Krymow V (1985) 'Group counselling for childen adopted at older ages', *Child Welfare* LXIV(2), pp 113–24.

Cunningham A and Cohen M (1985) 'Developing a post-adoption service in Essex', *Adoption & Fostering* 9:3, pp 44–6.

Dance C, Rushton A and Quinton D (2002) 'Emotional abuse in early childhood: relationships with progress in subsequent family placement', *Journal of Child Psychology and Psychiatry* 43:3, pp 395–407.

Deblinger E, Steer R and Lippman J (1999) 'Two year follow-up study of cognitive behavioural therapy for sexually abused children suffering post-traumatic stress symptoms', *Child Abuse and Neglect* 23, pp 1371–78.

Department of Health (1993) *Adoption: The Future*, London: Department of Health.

Department of Health (1997) *For Children's Sake Part II – An inspection of local authority post-placement and post-adoption services*, London: Social Services Inspectorate.

Department of Health (1998a) *Achieving the Right Balance*, LAC (98) 20, London; Department of Health.

Department of Health (1998b) *The Quality Protects Programme: Transforming children's services*, LAC (98) 28, London: Department of Health.

Department of Health (1999) *Framework for the Assessment of Children in Need and their Families*, London: Department of Health.

Department of Health (2000a) *Adopting Changes: Survey and inspection of local councils' adoption services*, London: Department of Health.

Department of Health (2000b) *Adoption Now: Messages from research*, Parker R, Ridgway J and Davies C (eds), Chapter 7 'Support', Chichester: Wiley.

Department of Health (2001a) *Adoption: Adoption and Permanence Taskforce Annual Report*, London: Department of Health.

Department of Health (2001b) *National Adoption Standards for England*, London: Department of Health.

Department of Health (2001c) *Adoption: Draft Practice Guidance to Support the National Adoption Standards for England – consultation* (consultation document), London: Department of Health.

Department of Health (2002a) *Children Looked After by Local Authorities Year Ending 31 March 2001*, London: Department of Health.

Department of Health (2002b) *Providing effective adoption support: A consultation document*, London: Department of Health.

Department of Health, Social Services and Public Safety (DHSSPS) (2001) *Adopting Best Care: Inspection of Statutory Adoption Services in Northern Ireland*.

Dozier M, Chase Stovall K, Albus K and Bates B (2001) 'Attachment for infants in foster care: the role of caregiver state of mind', *Child Development* 72:5, pp 1467–77.

Edwards C and Staniszewska S (2000) 'Accessing the user's perspective', *Health & Social Care in the Community*, 8, pp 417–42.

Egeland B, Sroufe A and Erikson M (1983) 'The developmental consequence of different patterns of maltreatment', *Child Abuse and Neglect* 7, pp 459–69.

Erich S and Leung P (1998) 'Factors contributing to family functioning of adoptive children with special needs: a long term outcome analysis', *Children & Youth Services Review* 20:1–2, pp 135–50.

Fahlberg V (1994) *A Child's Journey through Placement*, London: BAAF.

Fergusson D M, Lynskey M and Horwood L J (1995) 'The adolescent outcomes of adoption: A 16 year longitudinal study', *Journal of Child Psychology and Psychiatry and Allied Disciplines* 36:4, pp 597–615.

Fisher P A, Gunnar M R, Chamberlain P and Reid J B (2000) 'Preventive intervention for maltreated preschool children: Impact on children's behavior, neuroendocrine activity, and foster parent functioning', *Journal of the American Academy of Child & Adolescent Psychiatry* 39:11, pp 1356–64.

George C, Kaplan N and Main M (1996) *Adult Attachment Interview*, Unpublished Manuscript, Berkeley: University of California.

Ginsberg B G (1997) 'Training parents as therapeutic agents with foster/adoptive children using the Filian Approach', in Schaeffer J E and Briesmester J E, *Handbook of Parent Training Parents as Co-Therapists for Children's Behaviour Problems*, New York: John Wiley & Sons, pp 442–78.

Glaser D (2000) 'Child abuse and neglect and the brain – a review', *Journal of Child Psychology & Psychiatry* 41, pp 97–116.

Gordon C (1999) 'A parenting programme for parents of older children with disturbed attachment patterns', *Adoption & Fostering* 23:4, pp 49–56.

Groze V (1996) 'A one and two year follow-up study of adoptive families and special needs children', *Children and Youth Services Review* 18:1/2, pp 57–82.

Hanson R F and Spratt E G (2000) 'Reactive attachment disorder: what we know about the disorder and implications for treatment', *Child Maltreatment* 5:2, pp 137–45.

Hart A and Thomas H (2000) 'Controversial attachments: the indirect treatment of fostered and adopted children via Parent Co-Therapy', *Attachment & Human Development* 2:3, pp 306–27.

Hill M and Shaw M (eds) (1998) *Signposts in Adoption: Policy, practice and research issues*, London: BAAF.

Hodges J (1984) 'Two crucial questions: adopted children in psychoanalytic treatment', *Journal of Child Psychotherapy* 10, pp 47–56.

Hodges J and Steele M with Hillman S, Henderson K and Neil M (2000) 'Effects of abuse on attachment representations: narrative assessments of abused children', *Journal of Child Psychotherapy* 26:3, pp 422–55.

Hopkins J (2000) 'Overcoming a child's resistance to late adoption: how one new attachment can facilitate another', *Journal of Child Psychotherapy* 26:3, pp 335–47.

Howe D (1990a) 'The Post Adoption Centre: the first three years', *Adoption & Fostering* 14:1, pp 27–31.

Howe D (1990b) 'The consumer's view of the Post Adoption Centre', *Adoption & Fostering* 14:2, pp 32–6.

Howe D (1997) 'Parent-reported problems in 211 adopted children: some risk and protective factors', *Journal of Child Psychology and Psychiatry* 38:4, pp 401–11.

Howe D and Fearnley S (1999) 'Disorders of attachment and attachment therapy', *Adoption & Fostering* 23:2, pp 19–30.

Hughes B and Logan J (1995) 'The agenda for post-adoption services', *Adoption and Fostering* 19:1, pp 34–36.

Hughes D (1997) *Facilitating Developmental Attachment: The road to emotional recovery and behavioral change in foster and adopted children*, Northvale, NJ: Jason Aronson Inc.

Ivaldi G (2000) *Surveying Adoption: A comprehensive analysis of local authority adoptions 1998–9 (England)*, London: BAAF.

Jackson S (ed) (2002) *Nobody Ever Told Us School Mattered: Raising the educational attainments of children in care*, London: BAAF.

James B (1994) *Handbook for Treatment of Attachment-Trauma Problems in Children*, New York: Lexington Books.

Jernberg A (1993) *Attachment Formation*, Northvale, NJ: Jason Aronson.

Jewett C (1995) *Helping Children Cope with Separation and Loss*, London: Batsford Academic/BAAF.

Juffer F, Hoksbergen R A C, Riksen-Walraven J M and Kohnstamm G A (1997) 'Early intervention in adoptive families: supporting maternal sensitive responsiveness, infant-mother attachment, and infant competence', *Journal of Child Psychology & Psychiatry* 38:8, pp 1039–50.

Kaniuk J (1992) 'The use of relationship in the preparation and support of adopters', *Adoption & Fostering* 16:2, pp 47–52.

Katz L (1986) 'Parental stress and factors for success in older child adoption', *Child Welfare* LXV:6, pp 569–78.

Katz L (1999) 'Concurrent planning: benefits and pitfalls', *Child Welfare* 78, pp 71–87.

Keck G and Kupecky R (1995) *Adopting the Hurt Child*, Colorado Springs: Co. Pinon.

Kurtz Z (2001) 'Service innovation: learning from the 24 projects', *YoungMinds Magazine* 54, pp 31–3.

Levy T M (ed) (2000) *Handbook of Attachment Interventions*, London: Academic Press.

Logan J and Hughes B (1995) 'The agenda for post-adoption services', *Adoption & Fostering* 19:1, pp 34–6.

Lowe N (1997) 'The changing face of adoption – the gift/donation model versus the contract/services model', *Child and Family Law Quarterly* 9:4, pp 371–86.

Lowe N, Murch M, Borkowski M, Weaver A and Thomas C (1999) *Supporting Adoption: Reframing the approach*, London: BAAF.

Macaskill C (1985) 'Post-adoption support: is it essential?' *Adoption & Fostering* 9:1, pp 45–9.

Macaskill C (1986) 'Post adoption support', in Wedge P and Thoburn J (eds), *Finding Families for "Hard-to-place" Children: Evidence from research*, pp 40–50, BAAF.

Macaskill C (2002) *Safe Contact? Children in permanent placements and contact with their birth relatives*, Lyme Regis: Russell House Publishing.

Maluccio A, Fein E and Olmstead K (1986) *Permanency Planning for Children: Concepts and methods*, London: Routledge, Chapman & Hall.

MacMillan H and Munn C (2001) 'The sequelae of child maltreatment', *Current Opinion in Psychiatry* 14, pp 325–31.

Magee S and Thoday R (1995) 'How one local authority developed post-adoption services', *Adoption & Fostering* 19, pp 37–40.

Marcenko M O and Smith L K (1991) 'Post-adoption needs of families adopting children with developmental disabilities', *Children & Youth Services Review* 13:5–6, pp 413–24.

Mather M (2001) 'Adoption: The opportunity to give a child a second chance deserves health and social support', *BMJ (British Medical Journal)* 322, pp 1556–57.

Maughan B, Collishaw S and Pickles A (1998) 'School achievement and adult qualifications among adoptees: a longitudinal study', *Journal of Child Psychology & Psychiatry* 39:5, pp 669–86.

McDonald T, Propp J R and Murphy K C (2001) 'The post adoption experience: child, parent, and family predictors of family adjustment to adoption', *Child Welfare* 80:1, pp 71–94.

McGhee J (1995) 'Consumers' views of a post-placement support project', *Adoption & Fostering* 19:1, pp 41–5.

McRoy R (1999) *Special Needs Adoptions: Practice issues*, New York: Garland Publishing Inc.

Meezan W (1980) *Adoption Services in the States*, Washington, DC: US Department of Health and Human Services.

Minnis H and Devine C (2001) 'The effect of foster care training on the emotional and behavioural functioning of looked after children', *Adoption & Fostering* 25:1, pp 44–54.

Mulcahy J (1999) 'The value of post-adoption support services', *Adoption & Fostering* 23:6.

Myeroff R, Mertlich G and Gross J (1999) 'Comparative effectiveness of holding therapy with aggressive children', *Child Psychiatry and Human Development* 29, pp 303–13.

Neil E (2002) 'Contact after adoption: the role of agencies in making and supporting plans', *Adoption & Fostering* 26:1, pp 25–38.

Pallett C, Scott C, Blackeby K, Yule W and Weissman R (2002) 'Fostering changes: a cognitive-behavioural approach to help foster parents manage children', *Adoption & Fostering* 26:1, pp 39–48.

Parker R, Ridgway J and Davies C (eds) (1999) *Adoption Now: Messages from research*, Chichester: John Wiley & Sons.

Pecora P and Whittaker J K *et al* (2000) 'Adoption', in Gruyter A D, *The Child Welfare Challenge: Policy, practice and research*, New York.

Perry B (1995) *Maltreated Children: Experience, brain development and the next generation*, New York: WW Norton.

Peters B, Atkins M and McKay M (1999) 'Adopted children's behaviour problems: a review of five explanatory models', *Clinical Psychology Review* 19:3, pp 297–328.

Phillips R (1988) 'Post-adoption services: the views of adopters', *Adoption & Fostering* 14:2, pp 32–6.

Pinderhughes E E and Rosenberg, K F (1990) 'Family-bonding with high risk placements: a therapy model that promotes the process of becoming a family', *Formed Families: Adoption of children with handicaps*, New York: The Haworth Press, Inc., pp 209–30.

PIU (2000) *Prime Minister's Review of Adoption*, London: Cabinet Office.

Prevatt Goldstein B and Spencer M (2000) *Race and Ethnicity: A consideration of issues for black, minority ethnic and white children in family placement*, London: BAAF.

Quinton D, Rushton A, Dance C and Mayes D (1998) *Joining New Families: A study of adoption and fostering in middle childhood*, Chichester: John Wiley & Sons.

Roberts J (1996) 'Behavioural and cognitive-behavioural approaches', in Phillips R and McWilliam E (eds), *After Adoption: Working with adoptive families*, London: BAAF.

Rosenthal J A, Groze V and Morgan J (1996) 'Services for families adopting children via public child welfare agencies: use, helpfulness, and need', *Children & Youth Services Review* 18:1–2, pp 163–82.

Rowe J, Cain H, Hundleby M and Keane A (1984) *Long Term Foster Care*, London: Batsford Academic.

Rushton A (1989) 'Post-placement services for foster and adoptive parents – support, counselling or therapy?', *Journal of Child Psychology & Psychiatry* 30:2, pp 197–204.

Rushton A (1999) *Adoption as a Placement Choice: Arguments and evidence.* Maudsley Discussion Paper No. 9. Institute of Psychiatry, London.

Rushton A (2000) *Improving Post-Placement Support: Research into practice*, BAAF Research Symposium, London: BAAF.

Rushton A and Dance C (2002) 'Quality Protects: the Government's agenda', *Child and Adolescent Mental Health* 7:2, pp 60–5.

Rushton A and Dance C (in preparation) *Predictors of Outcome of Late Placed Adoptions: A longitudinal study.*

Rushton A, Dance C and Quinton D (2000) 'Findings from a UK-based study of late permanent placements', *Adoption Quarterly*, 3:3, pp 51–71.

Rushton A, Dance C, Quinton D and Mayes D (2001) *Siblings in Late Permanent Placement*, London: BAAF.

Rushton A, Mayes D, Dance C and Quinton D (in press) 'Parenting late placed children: the development of new relationships and the challenge of behavioural problems', *Journal of Clinical Child Psychology and Psychiatry.*

Rushton A, Quinton D and Treseder J (1993) 'New parents for older children: support services during eight years of placement', *Adoption & Fostering* 17:4, pp 39–45.

Rushton A, Treseder J and Quinton D (1988) *New Parents for Older Children*, London: BAAF.

Rushton A, Treseder J and Quinton D (1995) 'An 8-year prospective study of older boys placed in permanent substitute families', *Journal of Child Psychology and Psychiatry*, 36:4, pp 687–95.

Rutter M (1989) 'Age as an ambiguous variable in developmental research', *International Journal of Behavioural Development* 12, pp 23–51.

Rutter M (2000) 'Children in substitute care: some conceptual considerations and research implications', *Children & Youth Services Review* 22:9–10, pp 685–703.

Rutter M and O'Connor T G (1999) 'Implications of attachment theory for child care policies', in Cassidy J, *Handbook of Attachment: Theory, research and clinical applications*, New York: The Guildford Press, pp 823–44.

Salter A (2002) *The Adopter's Handbook: Information, resources and services for adoptive parents*, London: BAAF.

Sawbridge P (1990) 'Post-adoption counselling: what do we actually do?' *Adoption & Fostering* 14:1, pp 31–5.

Schore A (1996) 'The experience-dependent maturation of a regulatory system in the orbital prefrontal cortex and the origin of developmental psychopathology', *Development & Psychopathology* 8, pp 59–87.

Scottish Executive (2001) *For Scotland's Children* (The Stationery Office, Edinburgh), Edinburgh: The Scottish Office.

Scottish Office (1997) *Scotland's Children Volume 3 – Adoption and Parental Responsibilities Orders*, Edinburgh: The Scottish Office.

Selwyn J and Sturgess W (2001) *International Overview of Adoption – Policy and practice*, Bristol School for Policy Studies: University of Bristol.

Sinclair I and Gibbs I (1998) *Children's Homes: A study in diversity*, Chichester: John Wiley & Sons.

Skuse D and Bentovim A (1994) *Physical and Emotional Maltreatment*, Oxford: Blackwell Scientific Publications.

Smith S, Howard J and Monroe A (2000) 'Issues underlying behaviour problems in at-risk adopted children', *Children & Youth Services Review* 22:7, pp 539–62.

Smith S L and Howard J A (1999) *Promoting Successful Adoptions: Practice with troubled families*, Thousand Oaks, CA, US: Sage.

Stams G-J J, Juffer F, Van Ijzendoorn M H and Hoksbergen R A C (2001) 'Attachment-based intervention in adoptive families in infancy and children's development at age 7: two follow-up studies', *British Journal of Developmental Psychology* 19, pp 159–80.

Swaine J and Gilson J (1998) 'Meeting the needs of adoptive parents under stress: a group work approach', *Adoption & Fostering* 22:2, pp 44–53.

Thoburn J, Murdoch A and O'Brien A (1986) *Permanence in Child Care*, Oxford: Blackwell.

Thoburn J, Norford L and Rashid S (2000) *Permanent Family Placement for Children of Minority Ethnic Origin*, London: Jessica Kingsley Publishers.

Thomas C and Beckford V, Lowe N and Murch M (1999) *Adopted Children Speaking*, London: BAAF.

Triseliotis J (2002) 'Long term foster care or adoption? The evidence examined', *Child and Family Social Work* 7, pp 23–33.

Triseliotis J, Shireman J and Hundleby M (1997) *Adoption: Theory, policy and practice*, Cassell: London.

Warman A and Roberts C (2002) *Adoption and Looked After Children: International comparisons*, University of Oxford: Family Policy Briefing 1, Barnett House.

Watson L and McGhee J (1995) *Developing Post-Placement Support: A project in Scotland*, London: BAAF.

Webster-Stratton C and Hancock L (1998) 'Training for parents of young children with conduct problems: content, methods and therapeutic processes', in Schaefer C E and Briemeister J M (eds) *Handbook of parent training*, New York: John Wiley & Sons.

Welch M (1988) *Holding Time*, New York: Simon & Schuster.

Yates P (1995) 'Post-placement support for adoptive families of hard to place children', Unpublished MSc thesis, Edinburgh University.

Yeo P (1996) 'Adopted Adolescents and Their Families', in Phillips R and McWilliam E (eds) *After Adoption: working with adoptive families*, London: BAAF.

Yule W and Raynes N (1972) Behavioural characteristics of children in residential care in relation to indices of separation, *Journal of Child Psychology and Psychiatry* 13, pp 249–58.